"Ken Hemphill has wr_____ _____ ___ for discipleship. He has pr_ ___ a robust and readable biblical theology. It is an incredible resource for the mature Christian for personal growth as well as a ready resource for teaching and discipling others. Simply put, it is an intellectual and spiritual presentation of the Truth."

Will Hall
Vice President for News Services with the Southern Baptist Convention's Executive Committee and Executive Editor of Baptist Press

"In a society that is not only multicultural but also multidimensional in its religious expression it is imperative that Christian believers are clarion clear on the basic tenets of the Christian faith. In this book Ken Hemphill addresses some of the basic doctrines of the Christian faith in such an insightful manner that he echoes the sentiments of Jude, "Beloved, while I was very diligent to write to you concerning our common salvation, I found it necessary to write to you exhorting you to contend earnestly for the faith which was once for all delivered to the saints."

Dr. Walter Malone Jr.
Canaan Christian Church, Louisville, Kentucky

CORE CONVICTIONS

OTHER BOOKS BY KEN HEMPHILL

i BELIEVE

CORE CONVICTIONS
FOUNDATIONS OF FAITH

KEN HEMPHILL

Auxano
PRESS
Tigerville, South Carolina
www.AuxanoPress.com

Published by Auxano Press
Tigerville, South Carolina
www.AuxanoPress.com

Cover photo used with permission from The Cliffs Communities.

To order additional copies, contact Ken Hemphill,
Auxano Press, P.O. Box 315, Tigerville, SC 29688;
or order online to www.auxanopress.com.

For additional resources for this and other studies, go to
www.auxanopress.com or contact Ken Hemphill,
Auxano Press, P.O. Box 315, Tigerville, SC 29688.

I dedicate this book to:

Jim and Vicky Anthony

Friends whose courage, faith, generosity, and vision
challenge and inspire me and countless others
to "press on toward the goal for the prize
of the upward call of God in Christ Jesus"
(Philippians 3:14).

CONTENTS

Acknowledgments

The idea for this book was birthed in my heart as I sat with my good friend Walter Malone, the pastor of Canaan Christian Church. When I asked him about his preaching plans for the coming year, he indicated his desire to review the basic doctrines of the faith with his entire church family. I was convicted that a review of the foundational doctrines would profit all of us.

Studying God's Word always transforms one's life. This has certainly been true in this case as I have been deeply moved and challenged as I have attempted to provide a brief summary of 23 of the key doctrines of the Christian faith. I trust that your life will be impacted by God's Word as you read.

I am deeply indebted to my wife and partner in ministry who encourages me in my writing ministry. She provides the order and solitude in our home that allows me to reflect and write. Our devotional times together often provide the inspiration for ideas that will later find a place in my books.

My children and my grandchildren are my richest treasure. Tina and Brett have recently been blessed with a son, Micah Aydin, who is the delight of big sister Lois. Rachael and Trey are blessed with two "flaming redheads" who make life a delight. Katie and Daniel continue to grow in their faith as they parent Aubrey and Sloane. My family is the context of my ministry.

It is an honor to publish with Auxano Press whose ministry statement is to provide biblically sound tools to help individuals and their churches to experience balanced growth. Lawrence Kimbrough, my friend and colleague, has once again greatly enhanced my first draft. Thank you Christi Butler for your work on the art and the layout of the book. Judi Hayes provides wonderful guides for individual or group study which are available online at auxanopress.com.

I would like to take this opportunity to say a special word of thanks to Jim Anthony and The Cliffs for graciously proving the cover photo, featuring the chapel at The Cliffs at Glassy. The Cliffs offers a unique collection of eight communities, all minutes from one another, and all surrounded by hundreds of thousands of acres of protected parklands at the southernmost edge of the Blue Ridge Mountains. We are honored to make our home at The Cliffs Valley and have found solace in our beautiful surroundings.

For the sake of simplicity and brevity, I have used footnotes sparingly. I have been greatly helped by *The Holman Bible Dictionary*, Holman Bible Publishers; *New Dictionary of Theology*, InterVarsity Press; and J.I. Packer, *Concise Theology: A Guide to Historic Christian Beliefs*, Tyndale Publishers.

Free small group study guides for *Core Convictions* are available from AuxanoPress.com.

I pray that God will use this book of foundational truths to help you to live triumphantly with a life constructed on the solid rock.

Ken Hemphill
Travelers Rest, South Carolina
Spring 2010

FOREWARD

I remember well my first months of college life. Having sensed a call to vocational ministry, I enrolled in a Baptist college in my home state. Sitting in those first Old and New Testament classes, my faith was challenged as I realized there were views about God, the Bible, Jesus, salvation and other foundational truths that differed from those taught to me in my "growing up years" in Western North Carolina. During the months that followed, I realized those godly professors were not trying to destroy my faith, only make it stronger. My faith was challenged because I now had to declare not only "what" I believed, but "why" I believed it. God used the processing of my college and seminary years to bring me to a deepening understanding and embracing of the basic biblical truths that serve as the foundation of the Christian faith – truths I would be called upon to share with others for more than thirty years as a pastor/shepherd.

In *Core Convictions: Foundations of Faith*, Ken Hemphill helps the reader move from the "what" to the "why" of basic faith issues – bringing an encounter and hopefully a personal embracing of an unwavering biblical world view that impacts everything we think, say and do. For the past two years, I have had the privilege of walking beside Ken as we have led a small group for pastors at The Cliffs Valley Club, the community that he and Paula call home. What a joy to see the heart of a man who passionately desires that people "get it" – never content to simply parrot the "what" of faith, but to be deeply affected by the "why," moving nominal believers from the sidelines to living with joy and purpose in the middle of life's field.

As you "rehearse" the principals in these pages, you will have the opportunity to embrace and affirm your personal commitment to the transformational truths of God's Word, truths that should deeply affect the ways we see and live our lives. Enjoy the journey!

Rick Fisher
Foundation Director
The Cliffs Communities

INTRODUCTION

The small book you have in your hands was designed to help you understand some of the basic principles of Christian thought. This book begins with the issue of revelation and the Bible and concludes with the return of Christ and the ultimate realities of heaven and hell. Our goal is to develop a biblical understanding of what it means to be a Christian. Our purpose is not simply one of information but one of transformation. The understanding of these truths should form the basis for our Christian worldview.

A "worldview" is simply how we view the world and thus how we interpret and make value judgments about all the events of life. How do we make sense of our world and how do we find answers to the questions that really matter?

I was led to write this book because I have discovered that many believers do not think seriously about what it means to be a Christian. We trust in Christ for our eternal life, but we do not ask what it means to be a fully devoted follower of Christ. We do not ask what beliefs are encompassed by the commitment we have made.

After returning from Cambridge many years ago, I was privileged to teach for one year at Wingate Baptist College. At the time it was a junior college supported by Baptists of North Carolina. Students were required to take courses in the department of religion where I was teaching an overview of the Old Testament.

One day what I taught in the morning's lecture somehow piqued the interest of a particularly bright student. After class I asked him what had happened. He related that one of the pagan kings I had covered in my class lecture was also the topic in his history class the week before. He then declared that he was surprised that the Bible contained "real history." His comment was a stunning revelation for me. He had grown up in a conservative Baptist church. If someone had asked him about the Bible, he would have asserted that he believed it to be the Word of God. Why then did he need the evidence from a history class to confirm what he confessed to be true?

It dawned on me that when this student went to church or opened his Bible, it was as if he were stepping through the wardrobe in C. S. Lewis's Chronicles of Narnia story. What he learned from the Bible was true but in a parallel universe that didn't really connect to the universe of his real world represented by "real history." It is my firm belief that no book ever written has the significance of the Bible. It contains truth for all of life.

I have several goals for you—

> • To have greater confidence in your own faith commitment.

• To have a clearer understanding of what it means to be a follower of Christ.

• To be able to share with confidence the hope that is within you.

• To enjoy all that God has prepared for you.

Where do we start? The creation would be an obvious opening, but I have decided to begin with four essential sections on the Bible. If you do not have absolute confidence that the Bible you hold in your hands is the inspired, inerrant, infallible, and powerful Word of God, you will have little understanding or confidence in the other subjects covered in this book.

Read this book with an open mind and heart. Keep your Bible by your side. Look up the references and read them in context. Ask the Holy Spirit to give you understanding.

i Believe

IN THE BIBLE (REVELATION AND INSPIRATION)

CHAPTER 1

Many people claim to believe that God exists, but they pay little attention to what He says. Their professed knowledge doesn't translate into the next logical step. For if we believe God exists, we must ask whether He can be known and, if so, *how* He can be known? Then we must become accountable for what He has said.

A central teaching of Christianity is that God has chosen to reveal Himself to human beings—that He can be personally known, that He establishes relationship with us. This belief sets Christianity apart from most other world religions that chronicle man's attempts to find and appease God.

REVELATION

The Bible is the record of God's quest to make Himself known for the purpose of inviting people into dynamic, eternal relationship with Him. When Adam sinned in the garden, he did not seek God. As a matter of fact, he hid from God, thinking he could conceal his sin. Here's a wonderful truth: God sought Adam so that He could restore Adam's relationship with His Creator. God, out of His great love, has chosen to reveal Himself to man.

The stirring affirmation of Scripture is "Thus says the Lord." Through revelation God bridges the gap between Himself and humans, disclosing Himself and His will to His people.

The Bible, the written record of God's revelation of Himself, is crucial to our understanding of God, ourselves, and the world in which we live. The Bible is not simply important for adding information about God to our general knowledge. It is central to all knowledge, for in it we encounter the God who acts. The Bible is the most complete source of our knowledge about God; thus, all other truth must be measured against the truth of the Bible.

How would infinite God speak to finite humans? In Romans 1, Paul indicates that God reveals Himself in nature and through human conscience (vv. 19-20). We speak of such revelation as "general revelation." Yet God did not leave us to navigate our way with the light of general revelation alone. He provided "special revelation" about His redemptive work throughout history. He has shown us specifically how His love reached and is reaching mankind. The Bible is the record of God's special revelation.

When we use the word *revelation*, we are saying that the Bible's content originated with God. This was certainly the view of those who authored the various books of the Bible. David wrote: "The Spirit of the Lord spoke through me; his word was on my tongue" (2 Sam. 23:2 NIV). Jeremiah makes the same claim: "Then the Lord stretched out His hand and touched my mouth, and the Lord said to me, 'Behold, I have put My words in your mouth'" (Jer. 1:9).

Peter, speaking about Scripture, wrote: "Above all, you must understand that no prophecy of Scripture came about by the prophet's own interpretation. For prophecy never had its origin in the will of man, but men spoke from God as they were carried along by the Holy Spirit" (2 Pet. 1:20-21 NIV). In other words, the prophet did not initiate the conversation. It all started with God, reaching down, revealing, making Himself known.

INSPIRATION

The word *inspiration* means "God-breathed." It comes from the Latin word which means "to breathe in." Inspiration explains how the content of Scripture was communicated from God to man through human authors. Paul wrote, "All Scripture is God-breathed" (2 Tim. 3:16). This is what Peter meant, in the verse we considered above, when he wrote, "Men spoke from God as they were carried along by the Holy Spirit." The phrase "spoke from God" refers to revelation, and "carried along by the Holy Spirit" points to inspiration. Inspiration applies to the writing, preserving, and collecting of God's Word to His people.

This is vitally important: the Bible is not man's attempt to find or explain God; rather, it is God's revelation of Himself. God gave man the content, then inspired or guided him as he spoke and later recorded what God had revealed to him. God did not destroy the personality of the human authors but gave them the words, guided their writing, and protected them from error. Since they were human authors, they wrote in normal language, using figures of speech and illustrations common to their times and geographical locations.

We can view revelation and inspiration as a personal relationship between God the Holy Spirit and human writers, ensuring that the message was exactly what God intended to communicate to His people. Inspiration can be understood as a divine-human encounter whereby God reveals truth—a message from God to men communicated through men.

You can be confident that the Bible you have in your hands is a love letter whose content was given by God. Thus it is a reliable record of what God desires man to know about Him. It is therefore sufficient for life and practice.

FOR MEMORY AND MEDITATION
"For no prophecy was ever made by an act of human will, but men moved by the Holy Spirit spoke from God" (2 Pet. 1:21).

i BELIEVE

IN THE BIBLE (TRUSTWORTHY)

CHAPTER 2

Once we have determined that the Bible is God's revelation of Himself to man, we must ask if God revealed Himself in a trustworthy and accurate way. Perhaps you have heard someone say that the Bible is like other books in that it contains errors. If such were the case, then we would be forced to ask which portions of the Bible we could trust. We would need someone who could help us find the trustworthy passages. The affirmation of evangelical Christianity is that the Bible is truth without any mixture of error.

INFALLIBLE AND INERRANT

The question about the trustworthy nature of Scripture brings into our dialogue two important terms— *inerrancy* and *infallibility*. In classical usage, infallibility refers to a guide that is not deceived and does not deceive another. In other words, if you were hiking in an unfamiliar wilderness, you would hire a guide who knew the terrain well and would not be caught by surprise by bends or obstacles in the path. Further, you would want to know your guide was honest and would not intentionally lure you into danger.

The other term—inerrancy—speaks of information that is totally truthful and thus contains no mistakes. The historical position of the church is that when the

Bible is properly understood in the light of its ancient cultural form and content, it is absolutely truthful about God's will and God's way.[1]

TWO KEY QUESTIONS

I have found it helpful to ask and then answer two key questions when considering the trustworthiness and truthfulness of God's Word.

If God desired to reveal Himself to man, would He reveal Himself in a totally accurate (inerrant) and reliable (infallible) way? God, both by definition and by evidence, is not capricious or deceitful. If God were deceitful, man would have no hope of knowing Him since He is infinite and we are finite. We could not know when He was speaking truth or error. Ancient people had this problem with the pantheon of Roman and Greek gods who were often deceptive. But the God we encounter in the Bible is holy by nature and thus truthful and perfect. We can rightfully conclude that God would make Himself known in a way that is consistent with His perfect nature.

Could God protect and preserve a perfect revelation of Himself to mankind? Some people argue that we cannot have an inerrant text because God communicated His truth through fallible humans. They do not see how these messengers could avoid introducing errors into the text. If we accept the premise that God would reveal Himself perfectly, yet

---

1.   For additional information on inerrancy, see L. Russ Bush, *Understanding Biblical Inerrancy* (Fort Worth: Columbia, 1988).

we still contend there are errors in the text, then we are left with only one option: God desired to protect His Word but could not do so. This solution leaves us in the untenable position of believing that God is limited in what He is able to do.

The Bible reveals a God who created the world, came to earth in human flesh, and raised Jesus from the dead. Could He not also protect His written word from error? Could He not direct the mind of man whom He created? The answer is a resounding "Yes!"

When we have an inerrant and infallible record of God's communication with man, we are able to speak with confidence on issues of life and eternity. When inerrancy is rejected, however, we become less sure of Scripture's authority, less certain of our own faith, and more susceptible to alternative views.

WHAT ABOUT ALL THE DIFFICULTIES?
Sometimes Christians are confronted with the charge that the Bible contains errors and inconsistencies. Many such objections arise from immaterial and uninformed impressions. People who make such claims typically do so because of exposure to negative attitudes about the Bible from others rather than their own investigation of its contents. Archaeological evidence continually confirms the historical accuracy of Scripture. The writers of Scripture made reference to numerous historical events that could have been easily checked by their contemporaries. If the Bible contained historical inaccuracies, why did those who

were contemporary with the authors not discredit their writings?

Many of the objections to inerrancy are based on the use of figures of speech or symbolic numbers. Critics wonder, "Do you really believe that the trees clapped their hands?" (See Isa. 55:12). Such suggestions are meaningless. Figures of speech do not constitute an error any more than they do in modern speech. Do people believe that thoughts literally "pop" into their heads or their hearts actually "sink" when they're sad?

Jesus Himself regarded the Scriptures as trustworthy. He said, for example, "It is easier for heaven and earth to pass away than for one stroke of a letter of the Law to fail" (Luke 16:17). On one occasion Jesus was accused of blasphemy. His only defense was to refer to the Scriptures and declare, "The Scripture cannot be broken" (John 10:35b).

You can read you Bible with absolute confidence that it accurately conveys God's Word.

FOR MEMORY AND MEDITATION
"It is easier for heaven and earth to pass away than for one stroke of a letter of the Law to fail" (Luke 16:17).

i BELIEVE

IN THE BIBLE (PRESERVATION)

CHAPTER 3

Another question remains. It is not enough to assert that the original documents (sometimes called the *autographs*) were accurate; we must also know whether the Bible has been preserved with fidelity from generation to generation. Many Muslims contend that the original text has been corrupted over the years through transmission.

Some have argued that the early church actually distorted the Gospels, rewriting them to create their own story. In other words, they made Jesus more Godlike to preserve the movement we call early Christianity. This suggestion has been the theme of several popular movies.

Such a suggestion is not based on any historical evidence. Christians were widely mistrusted and persecuted during the latter part of the first century. If there had been any attempt to alter the life and teachings of Jesus, eyewitnesses both inside and outside the Christian movement would have immediately cried foul. Further, it is difficult to be convinced that early believers would joyfully face martyrdom for what they knew to be a manufactured story.

RELIABILITY OF THE DOCUMENTS

Both the quantity and quality of the manuscripts of the Scripture give us confidence in the faithful preservation of the Bible. In the case of the Old Testament, the Hebrew texts are unusually well-preserved. They have proved to be exceptionally reliable, a fact that has gained additional support by the discovery of the Dead Sea Scrolls. W. F. Albright, late professor emeritus of John Hopkins University and noted archaeologist, affirmed: "There can be no doubt that archaeology has confirmed the substantial historicity of Old Testament tradition."

With more than five thousand Greek manuscripts and eight thousand Latin manuscripts, no other book in ancient literature can compare with the New Testament in terms of documentary support. For example, we have discovered only seven ancient copies of Plato's writings, five of Aristotle's, and 634 of Homer's. College professors will teach Aristotle and Homer without ever raising a question as to the reliability of the text they hold in their hands. Yet these same professors will cast doubt on the reliability of the Bible.

We must take into account the great reverence the Jewish scribes and early Christians had for the Scriptures. They believed they were preserving the very Word of God; therefore, they exercised extreme caution in accurately copying and preserving the authentic text.

If you have a study Bible, you may occasionally see a note in the margin or at the bottom of the page that provides an alternative reading for a word or verse.

These variant readings were usually the result of an auditory or visual error in the copying process. Most relate to issues no more significant than a spelling error. Only a small number would alter in any way the understanding of the text. And absolutely none of them call into question a major doctrinal or factual teaching.

Sir William Ramsay, a wealthy atheist with a doctorate in philosophy from Oxford University, devoted his life to archaeological research with a desire to disprove the Bible. After twenty-five years of work, he became so impressed with the historical accuracy of Luke-Acts that he shocked the world by declaring himself to be a Christian. You can be confident the Bible you hold has been accurately preserved.

CANONIZATION
Let's consider one final question about the reliability of the Bible. Are there any books that should be added to the sixty-six we have in our Bible? The Greek word *kanon* referred to the rod of straightness from which measurements could be made. The term *canonization*, when applied to the Bible, means the establishment of the books that are considered to be authentically inspired and thus accepted as the Word of God.

You may have picked up a Bible that includes books included after the Old Testament called the Apocrypha, which means "hidden things." While these books shed valuable light on the period of time between the Old and New Testament, evangelicals do not consider them as having the authority of Scripture. By the time of Jesus, agreement on the canon of the Old Testament was widespread. The Jewish elders meeting at Jamnia around A.D. 70 were in general agreement on the books that comprised the Old Testament.

The acceptance of the Hebrew canon of Scripture as authoritative by the early church exercised great influence on the formation of the New Testament canon. They continued to read regular portions of the Old Testament as part of their worship. Soon they added the teachings of Jesus. The teachings of the apostles were especially valued, particularly as the eyewitnesses to Jesus' time on earth began to die.

The canon of New Testament Scripture was set out in Athanasius' Easter Letter (A.D. 367), containing the twenty-seven books to the exclusion of all others. A similar list was confirmed by the Synod of Carthage in A.D. 397. We can trust that God has led His people throughout history to recognize the writings He intended to be authoritative, the ones that comprise our Bible.

FOR MEMORY AND MEDITATION
"Your word I have treasured in my heart, that I may not sin against You" (Ps. 119:11).

i BELIEVE

IN THE BIBLE (AUTHORITY AND POWER)

When we read a great classic or a powerful poem, we may be moved to tears or be inspired to do more to ensure that our life counts. The Bible, however, has the power to transform a person's life. No other book has had so great an impact on humankind through the centuries. You could marshal countless testimonies from people who will tell you that reading the Bible changed their lives.

TESTIMONY CONCERNING ITS POWER

The testimony of the authority and power of Scripture is found in both the Old and New Testaments. Isaiah wrote: "So will My word be which goes forth from My mouth; it will not return to Me empty, without accomplishing what I desire, and without succeeding in the matter for which I sent it" (55:11). If you read this verse in context, you will discover that God tells Isaiah that His ways and thoughts are higher than those of any mortal. He then compares His words to the rain and snow which waters the earth and causes seed to sprout. The Word has power to accomplish what God intended when He spoke it through the prophet. You can be assured that your study of God's Word will change your life.

Paul, writing to the Romans, declared: "I am not ashamed of the gospel, for it is the power of God for salvation to everyone who believes, to the Jew first and also to the Greek" (1:16). The power of the gospel is not dependent on Paul or any other human agent. It exercises its own power. This truth should give you great confidence as you share your testimony plus Scripture with a non-Christian friend.

The writer to the Hebrews makes a similar observation: "The word of God is living and active and sharper than any two-edged sword, and piercing as far as the division of soul and spirit, of both joints and marrow, and able to judge the thoughts and intentions of the heart" (4:12). Have you ever been reading the Bible when a certain verse captures your attention, as though it was written just for you at just this moment in your life? You may have read it multiple times before, but today it seems like you're discovering it for the first time. It explodes from the page and burrows deeply into your heart. That is the power of Scripture as the Holy Spirit who inspired its writing applies it to your heart and mind.

You may then wonder what the Word accomplishes in the life of the believer. When Paul wrote to his young protégé Timothy, he encouraged him to continue in the things he had learned and about which he had developed strong conviction. He speaks of Timothy studying the Scriptures (a reference to the Old Testament) which gave him the wisdom leading to salvation through Christ. He then declares: "All Scripture is inspired by God and profitable for teaching, for reproof, for correction, for training in righteousness; so that the man of God may be adequate, equipped for every good work" (2 Tim. 3:16-17). Just look at the power of God's Word. It teaches, convicts, corrects, and trains in righteousness, enabling you to accomplish anything God calls you to do. Do you understand now why personal and corporate Bible study is so essential to Christian growth?

ONE OF A KIND

The Bible—what a book! It was uniquely produced, involving more than forty authors who wrote independently of one another over a span of more than fifteen centuries. These authors included kings, shepherds, a tax collector, a fisherman, a Pharisee turned believer, and a physician, among others. Their diversity, reflected in their educational levels and socioeconomic lifestyles, is evident in their writings. Virtually every known literary form is found in the Bible. Yet it has a central theme and a consistent, continuous message from beginning to end. The only explanation for such unity and consistency is that a single divine author spoke through the various human authors.

No other book can compare with the Bible in terms of sales and influence. It remains a best-seller year after year. More books are written about the Bible than any other book—either to explain it or explain it away. It stands at the center of the literary world. It has been banned and burned and subjected to destructive criticism, and yet it remains. It remains because it has power and authority. It is not just another holy book.

The Bible, unlike any other writing, has the power to change a person's life. You must allow the Bible to be authoritative as it speaks to you about issues of life and eternity. As you read your Bible, invite the Holy Spirit to help you understand it and apply it to your own situation. You will find it convicting, correcting, and encouraging you—yes, changing you.

FOR MEMORY AND MEDITATION

"All Scripture is inspired by God and profitable for teaching, for reproof, for correction, for training in righteousness" (2 Tim. 3:16).

i BELIEVE

IN GOD

History begins with God. The first statement of the Bible reflects this fundamental truth: "In the beginning God created the heavens and the earth" (Gen. 1:1). In the last chapter of the Bible, God declares, "I am the Alpha and the Omega, the first and the last, the beginning and the end" (Rev. 22:13).

God is unique. No person, object, or idea can be compared to Him. The challenge we have in explaining or fully comprehending God is that He is beyond our finite minds. Anything we say about God is based on His self-revelation. The limitation of human vocabulary forces us to express infinite God in finite language and images.

OUR UNDERSTANDING OF GOD AFFECTS OUR THINKING

God is the primary subject of the Bible. The doctrine of God is a fundamental axiom of evangelical thought, and our understanding of Him should affect our thinking and our values. As God's creation, we are accountable to God. And just because our limitations make it impossible for us either to prove or disprove the existence of God by human reason alone, we are no less obliged to align our lives with His will. God precedes and exceeds science. When someone suggests that God does not exist, he does not do away with God or his responsibilities before God. He merely gives Godlike qualities to an impersonal universe.

But the God who reveals Himself in Scripture is unlike the "god concept" in most other world religions. Instead of adopting a concept that sees man attempting to reach up from the world to god, Scripture moves in the direction from God to the world. God existed apart from His world. He created it and makes Himself known through self-revelation. He comes to us.

The personal name Yahweh (Jehovah) is commonly translated "Lord," but it is actually the Hebrew verb "to be," and could be translated "I am who I have always been." This indicates both His eternality and His self-existence (see Exod. 3:14). As Israel traveled among the nations in Old Testament times, they were confronted by the plurality of deities in the surrounding world. They began to comprehend that Yahweh was neither a tribal god nor a regional deity but the one true God who fashioned the world and ruled over all nations and peoples. This understanding became the heart of their mission—the calling that Israel had been selected by God to bless the nations. The clear expression of the monotheistic belief of Israel is expressed in the fundamental confession of faith called the *Shema*, recorded in Deuteronomy 6:4: "Hear, O Israel! The Lord is our God, the Lord is one!"

When Israel was overthrown and forced into Babylonian captivity, the worship of Yahweh would have disappeared if He were understood to be a tribal god and the captivity to be merely a natural event. But captivity was no natural event. The God of Israel was in complete control of history, reigning supreme over all nations. Isaiah asserts Yahweh's lordship over the nations of the earth and His control over history: "'I, even I, am the Lord, and there is no savior besides Me. It is I who have declared and saved and proclaimed, and there was no strange god among you; so you are My witnesses,' declares the Lord, 'and I am God. Even from eternity I am He, and there is none who can deliver out of My hand; I act and who can reverse it?'" (43:11-13).

OLD TESTAMENT UNDERSTANDING IS THE BASIS FOR NEW TESTAMENT

The Old Testament understanding of God is the basis for everything the New Testament writers teach. The God of Abraham, Isaac, and Jacob is now revealed in Jesus the Christ. Because God became flesh in Christ, we now have a new level of intimacy in our relationship with God. We are privileged to address God as Father (Matt. 6:9; cf. Rom. 8:15). The personal presence of God in Christ is both the normative and complete source of knowledge about God (Heb. 1:1-3).

We often speak of God with words and phrases that begin with *omni-*, indicating that He is beyond temporal limitations. These indicate both His eternality and His immensity. We use the term *omnipresence*, for example, to indicate His abiding and permanent presence. *Omnipotence* refers to His power to accomplish His purposes and carry out His will in the world. *Omniscience* indicates that He knows everything. *Omni-benevolence* tells us that God is altogether good and giving.

The most basic word to describe God is *holy*, which includes the idea of righteousness and purity. Holy God is set above all else in majesty, power, authority, and love. He is eternal. He is spirit. He has none of the limitations connected with material form. God is love, and love is the primary motivation behind His self-revelation (John 3:16). God reveals Himself as Father. He is Father of all persons by virtue of creation (Ps. 68:5), He is Father of believers by means of redemption/adoption (Gal. 3:26), and He is uniquely the Father of Jesus Christ by incarnation (Matt. 11:25-27).

God is intimate and knowable. He is not an impersonal force like gravity; He is living, working in His world, and relating to His people. He forms relationships with us. He has purpose and will. He is God, and there is no other.

FOR MEMORY AND MEDITATION
"I am the Alpha and the Omega, the first and the last, the beginning and the end" (Rev. 22:13).

i BELIEVE

IN JESUS

CHAPTER 6

Our knowledge of God is based entirely on God's
self-revelation. The Bible tells us that He is self-evident
in His creation; therefore, we have no excuse for not
acknowledging Him as Maker (Rom. 1:20). The focal
truth of Scripture is that God's supreme revelation of
Himself occurred when He sent His only begotten
Son—One sharing the unique essence of the
Father—for the redemption of all people (John 3:16).
Everything in Scripture points to this overwhelming
truth: Jesus Christ is the Son of God. He is the clearest
picture of God the world has ever seen. As Jesus said,
"He who has seen Me has seen the Father" (John 14:9).

The name *Jesus* is the Greek form of *Joshua*, which
means "Yahweh is salvation." The title *Christ* means
"anointed"—a designation given to Jesus by the Father
and affirmed by His followers who acknowledged Him
to be the long-awaited Messiah. This title gathers up
all the Old Testament prophetic hopes for a redeemer
and infuses them with new meaning in Jesus.

THE EARLY YEARS

Two Gospels give us a record of Jesus' birth and
infancy. He was born in Bethlehem of Judea—the
location prophesied in Micah 5:2 (Matt. 2:6)—toward
the end of Herod's reign (37-4 B.C.). He spent his

boyhood and youth in Nazareth, along with His four brothers and some sisters fathered by Joseph, a carpenter, and his wife, Mary. Mary was a virgin at the time of Jesus' conception and remained so until Jesus was born (Matt. 1:18). His early life up to age thirty is not chronicled, apart from Luke's record of a visit to Jerusalem at age twelve.

But the story of Jesus begins long before Bethlehem. John opens his Gospel by looking back to eternity past. "In the beginning was the Word, and the Word was with God, and the Word was God . . . And the Word became flesh, and dwelt among us . . . No one has seen God at any time; the only begotten God who is in the bosom of the Father, He has explained Him" (John 1:1, 14, 18). Jesus is fully God! Jesus and God are one! Jesus fully explains God! Our God is an awesome God!

PUBLIC MINISTRY

Jesus' first public appearance was His baptism near Jericho at the hands of John the Baptist. The descent of the dove at His baptism signified that He was the one anointed by God to be the Servant-Messiah (Isa. 61:1; Matt. 3:17). The words from heaven indicated He was God's Son and Israel's king.

The main phase of His public ministry began in Galilee after John the Baptist's imprisonment by Herod Antipas (Mark 1:14). Jesus' miracles were the mighty works of God, testifying that He was the Prophet sent by God (John 6:14). His teaching was unlike other earthly teachers. "Never has a man spoken the way this man speaks" (John 7:46). His teaching had such authority that people recognized He was speaking from God. His primary theme was the kingdom of God. He declared that the kingdom had begun in His ministry but would not come to fullness until His final return. To help people understand heavenly truths, He spoke in parables. Most of these were about the kingdom—what it was like, what kingdom life was like, and how one could enter it.

HIS DEATH AND RESURRECTION

His life ended with crucifixion, a ritual murder engineered by religious leaders but carried out by Roman authorities. Yet His life was not taken but given. He died to forgive the sins of mankind and to redeem lost people for Himself. The early church understood and consistently proclaimed that the death of Christ was God's plan for redeeming the world. Paul connects Jesus' death with the sacrificial system of the Old Testament, declaring that His death was a sacrifice for others (Eph. 5:2).

His death was followed by His glorious resurrection on the first day of the week. He was raised bodily from the grave and thus overcame the curse of sin, granting life to those who would live in relationship with Him (1 Cor. 15). He sits now at the right hand of the Father, pouring out blessings on His church.

Several key truths about Jesus are essential to the Christian worldview. (1) *Jesus is fully God*. Paul indicates that Jesus existed before creation and was active in it (Col. 1:15-17). Only God could be described in such terms. (2) *Jesus was fully man*. He did not merely pretend to be man. He felt all the emotions and was tested in every way man can be tested, yet he did not sin (Heb. 4:15). Certainly the full deity and humanity of Jesus are truths beyond human comprehension, but God is not bound by the limits of human reason. (3) *Jesus died a substitutionary death*, meaning its effects apply to the lives of others (Heb. 9:12, 15). (4) *He rose from the dead*, an event corroborated by numerous witnesses (1 Cor. 15). (5) *He is Lord* (Phil. 2:9-11). (6) *He will return in triumph*.

FOR MEMORY AND MEDITATION
"And the Word became flesh, and dwelt among us, and we saw His glory, glory as of the only begotten from the Father, full of grace and truth" (John 1:14).

i BELIEVE

IN THE HOLY SPIRIT

The Holy Spirit is the third person of the Triune God. He is not merely a vague, impersonal, ambiguous force. He is alive! The Holy Spirit is God and has thus been active from before time began.

OLD TESTAMENT

The term *Holy Spirit* occurs only twice in the Old Testament (Ps. 51:11; Isa. 63:10-11), but references to the Spirit of God are plentiful. He was active in creation, moving over the surface of the waters (Gen. 1:2). The Spirit is sometimes pictured as a mighty wind, signifying the invisible and mysterious power of God. The Hebrew word *ruach* means wind, breath, or spirit. The Spirit as a mighty wind can part the waters of the Red Sea (Exod. 15:10) or animate the dry bones of Israel (Ezek. 37:9, 14).

The Spirit can manifest Himself in and through people. The Spirit enabled Joseph to interpret Pharaoh's dream (Gen. 41:38). He inspired the prophets. David declares, "The Spirit of the Lord spoke through me" (2 Sam. 23:2 NIV). When the Spirit of the Lord "came upon" men like Othniel, Sampson, or Jephthah, they were able to lead Israel (cf. Judg. 3:10). The Spirit gave men knowledge, wisdom, understanding, and craftsmanship abilities to build the tabernacle (Exod. 31:3). His power was manifest as Israel went into battle. Thus Zechariah warns Zerubbabel, "'Not by might nor by power, but by My Spirit,' says the Lord of hosts" (Zech. 4:6).

But the Spirit's work in the Old Testament is usually an individual, sporadic, and temporary manifestation of power for a unique task. The idea of His indwelling presence for ministry was yet to come.

A VISION OF THE FUTURE

When Moses was overwhelmed by the task of leading Israel, God placed a portion of his Spirit upon the elders. This increased the number of those equipped to operate with God's revealed wisdom and power. Still, Moses longed for the day when God would place His Spirit on all His people (Num. 11:29). Later prophets like Joel, Ezekiel, and Isaiah spoke of a day when the Spirit would be available to all God's people, living in them and enabling them to obey God's Word, empowering them for service. The reception of the Spirit would be based on repentance, requiring a new heart.

"I will put My Spirit within you and cause you to walk in My statutes, and you will be careful to observe My ordinances" (Ezek. 36:27). "I will pour out My Spirit on your offspring" (Isa. 44:3). The early church saw the events surrounding Pentecost as a fulfillment of Joel's promise: "I will pour out My Spirit on all mankind; and your sons and daughters will prophesy, your old men will dream dreams, your young men will see visions" (Joel 2:28).

NEW TESTAMENT

The New Testament opens with an outbreak of Spirit activity. A priest named Zacharias is told in a vision that he will have a son who will be filled with the Holy Spirit while yet in his mother's womb (Luke 1:15-17). The angel tells Mary that the Holy Spirit will come upon her and she will give birth to the Son of God (Luke 1:35). When Elizabeth hears Mary's greeting at her door, she is filled with the Spirit and pronounces Mary blessed of God (Luke1:41-42). Zacharias (Luke 1:67), Simeon (Luke 2:25), and Anna (Luke 2:36) prophesy concerning Jesus, being inspired and directed by the Holy Spirit.

Many of the early events of Spirit activity resemble those of the Old Testament. The turning point is the anointing of Jesus by the Spirit (Luke 3:22). Jesus is the first man to be indwelt by the Spirit, and thus He is the prototype of what it means to be Spirit filled. When John the Baptist saw the Spirit remain upon Jesus, he knew this was the one who would baptize in the Spirit (John 1:33).

Jesus instructs Nicodemus that he must be born of the Spirit (John 3:4-9)—the One who is the source of the new birth. The Spirit incorporates believers into the body of Christ (1 Cor. 12:13). Paul writes of the Spirit's indwelling the believer and declares, "If anyone does not have the Spirit of Christ, he does not belong to Him" (Rom. 8:9b). The baptism of the Spirit, rightly understood, occurs at the moment of salvation when He incorporates us into the body of Christ.

The Spirit indwells believers (Rom. 8:9), gives life to our physical bodies (Rom. 8:11), gives us inner assurance that we are sons and heirs (Rom. 8:16-17), helps our weaknesses (Rom. 8:26), and intercedes for us in prayer (Rom. 8:27). Discussing His impending departure, Jesus told the disciples it was to their advantage that He leave them physically since He would send them the Holy Spirit when He went away.

The book of Acts begins with the promise of the Spirit (Acts 1:8) and the descent of the Spirit at Pentecost (Acts 2:1-13). Paul writes extensively about the Holy Spirit. He teaches that the Spirit produces the character of Christ (fruit of the Spirit, Gal. 5:22-23) in the lives of believers and empowers them for service through gifts of the Spirit (1 Cor. 12-14; Rom. 12; Eph. 4). He challenges all believers to be continually filled with the Holy Spirit (Eph. 5:18).

FOR MEMORY AND MEDITATION
"For by one Spirit we were all baptized into one body" (1 Cor. 12:13).

i BELIEVE

IN THE TRIUNE GOD

How do we articulate the truth that God is simultaneously one and three? God is so much greater than our finite understanding, we cannot fully comprehend the idea of "three in one," nor can we express it with our limited vocabulary. Nevertheless, we can affirm that the idea is clearly taught in Scripture.

OLD TESTAMENT

The Old Testament teaches the oneness and uniqueness of God. Israel's confession of faith, the *Shema*, states it thus: "Hear, O Israel! The Lord is our God, the Lord is one!" (Deut. 6:4). Nonetheless, the concept of the triune nature of God is implied in the Old Testament. The Spirit of God was active in creation (Gen. 1:2; Ps. 104:30). The Word of God is also spoken of as an agent of creation (Ps. 33:6, 9). Who is this Word? John begins the prologue to his Gospel by helping us understand "the Word became flesh" in Jesus Christ (John 1:14).

NEW TESTAMENT

The doctrine of the triune God develops as the early Christian community responded to the teachings of Jesus and attempted to account for how they experienced God through His Son, as well as through the ongoing infilling of His Spirit. The New Testament confirms the monotheistic faith of the Old Testament but expands it to cover the coming of Jesus and the outpouring of the Holy Spirit.

At the baptism of Jesus, we first encounter the three persons of the triune God ministering at one moment. The Son is baptized by the Spirit, and the Father affirms the Son. "He saw the heavens opening, and the Spirit like a dove descending upon Him; and a voice came out of the heavens: 'You are My beloved Son'" (Mark 1:10-11).

The disciples, who had witnessed Jesus praying to His Father, were invited to pray to the Father in the name of Jesus the Son. Belief in Jesus' divinity is clearly stated in the New Testament, and thus worship of Him as God becomes fundamental to New Testament Christianity. In Philippians 2, Paul speaks of the preexistence of Christ who existed in the form of God and yet laid aside heavenly prerogative to become man. He was highly exalted by God, given a name above all names, prompting all to worship Him (5-11).

The "farewell discourses" of Jesus in John 14–16 must have had a profound impact on the understanding that God manifest Himself in three distinct yet equal persons. Jesus comforted His followers by promising them that He was preparing a place for them in His Father's house (14:1-4). He speaks of His unity with the Father: "I am in the Father, and the Father is in Me" (14:10). He promises that upon His departure, He will ask the Father to send "another

Helper" (14:16). Jesus was the first Helper, but after His departure another Helper would be sent who would be counselor, advocate, comforter, and interpreter. This Helper came in the person of the Holy Spirit at Pentecost. The Spirit is the agent of God active in the continuing ministry of the Son (16:12-15).

THE ONGOING WORK OF THE CHURCH
The resurrected Lord commissioned His church to complete His work by making disciples of the nations. Further, He prescribed baptism to be administered "in the name of the Father and the Son and the Holy Spirit" (Matt. 28:19). "Name" is singular, indicating that God is One and yet He expresses Himself as Father, Son, and Holy Spirit.

In two different passages where Paul discusses gifts for ministry, he indicates that God in His triune nature is at work. "Now there are varieties of gifts, but the same Spirit. And there are varieties of ministries, and the same Lord. There are varieties of effects, but the same God who works all things in all persons" (1 Cor. 12:4-6). In Ephesians he declares, "There is one body and one Spirit . . . one Lord . . . one God and Father of all who is over all and through all and in all" (4:4-6). The unity of God both illustrates and empowers the unity necessary for the ministry of the church.

But language concerning the triune God is not limited to the writings of Paul. Peter speaks of the ministry of all three persons in the redemption of the believers in Asia, how they were chosen "according to the foreknowledge of God the Father, by the sanctifying work of the Spirit, to obey Jesus Christ and be sprinkled with His blood" (1 Pet. 1:2). John begins the book of Revelation with an expanded Trinitarian formula in his prayer for grace and peace from the Father, the Spirit, and Jesus Christ.

Here is a simple statement that might help us as we try to grasp a concept clearly beyond comprehension. God the Father is the *only* God there will ever be; God the Son is the *only* God we will ever see; God the Spirit is the *only* God living in me.

FOR MEMORY AND MEDITATION
It is appropriate that we end with Paul's Trinitarian blessing: "The grace of the Lord Jesus Christ, and the love of God, and the fellowship of the Holy Spirit, be with you all" (2 Cor. 13:14).

i BELIEVE

IN CREATION

"In the beginning God created the heavens and the earth" (Gen. 1:1). "In the beginning" is not an introductory phrase like "Once upon a time." It is a solemn affirmation that God created everything from nothing. The repeated phrase "Let there be" indicates that He called everything into being with intentionality and purpose.

When we observe the complex and uniquely balanced world, we are led to conclude that an intelligent designer was at work. When we look at human life, we might further conclude that the designer is personal and moral. The Bible clearly declares the truth that God is all powerful and yet intensely personal, desiring to be known by those He has created. The brief account in Genesis is less concerned with questions of "how" and "when" than with "who" and "why." While it contains reliable scientific affirmations, its focus is on theology rather than geology or biology.

CREATION REVEALS GOD

In writing to the Romans, Paul declares: "For since the creation of the world His invisible attributes, His eternal power and divine nature, have been clearly seen, being understood through what has been made, so that they are without excuse" (Rom. 1:20). From this and other Scriptures we can learn several key truths:

God alone is infinite Creator. He is the uncaused Cause. Everything owes its existence to Him. The writer of Hebrews affirms this truth: "By faith we understand that the worlds were prepared by the word of God, so that what is seen was not made out of things which are visible" (Heb. 11:3). God is not dependent on anything, yet everything is dependent on Him. God did not need creation to complete Him, and thus we can understand that He created the world with purpose, based on His love.

The entire creation is good. In the Genesis account the repeated phrase "It was good" indicates that each creative act was exactly what God intended. Every event of creation corresponded to His eternal purpose and thus has been given appropriate value by its Creator. The world was created for the habitation of man and woman, who are to be its caretakers. This provides the objective basis for ecological concern.

God created humans male and female in His own image. Any worldview that suggests man is nothing more than the product of chance mutation and natural selection attaches little value to human life. Men and women were intentionally created by God as rational, relational, and responsible beings. We were created in God's image as spiritual beings, designed to live in relationship with our Creator.

God continues to care for His creation. Genesis 2:5-6 mentions cultivating and watering the ground. God established natural laws so nature would be sustained with continuity, regularity, and predictability (Gen. 1:14; Ps. 74:16-17). Men like Bacon, Galileo, Copernicus, Kepler, and Kelvin—the fathers of modern science—based their theories on the conviction that God created the universe and operated it though observable laws.

God alone establishes reality. God creates outside Himself and thus grants reality to created beings. Finite beings are dependent on their infinite Creator. God grants man freedom that must be exercised within the context of His moral absolutes. This means that men are accountable to the Creator by exercising their divinely granted freedom. Man's greatest need is to know and cooperate with the laws of God revealed in nature and in the Bible. These truths will lead man ultimately to Christ.

THE IMPLICATIONS OF OUR VIEW OF CREATION

1. Creation witnesses to God's existence and sovereignty (2 Pet. 3:5).

2. Creation means that the "created" is accountable to the Creator. This truth forms the basis for moral values. Adam was given free choice and was then held accountable for his choice (Gen. 2:16-17).

3. The dignity and sacredness of human life are affirmed by the truth that man is created in God's image.

4. Creation by a personal God affirms that humans are relational beings. This should determine how we treat other persons created in God's image.

5. The incarnation—God becoming flesh and dwelling among us—is wholly consistent with the biblical view of creation.

6. Creation gives humans an important role as caretakers of the created world.

7. Creation affirms God's providential care for His creation. He remains actively involved in sustaining the creation.

8. Creation provides the structure for family, church, and society (1 Cor. 11:1-16; 1 Tim. 2:8-15).

9. Bodily resurrection is consistent with the biblical view of the world (1 Cor. 15:45-49).

10. The second coming of the Lord for judgment and redemption is based on a biblical view of creation (2 Pet. 3:3-13).

FOR MEMORY AND MEDITATION

"By faith we understand that the worlds were prepared by the word of God, so that what is seen was not made out of things which are visible" (Heb. 11:3).

i BELIEVE

CHAPTER 10

GOD MADE HUMANS IN HIS IMAGE

The statement recorded in Genesis 1:27—"God created man in His own image"—indicates that humans are like God in a manner that no other earthly creatures are. This means we have the opportunity of relating to Him and replicating at an earthly level the holy ways of God. It means that all human life is sacred and that each of us is created with purpose.

LIVING BEING

"The Lord God formed man of dust from the ground, and breathed into his nostrils the breath of life; and man became a living being" (Gen. 2:7). Man, created from the dust of the earth, has a material body that is given life by a nonmaterial, personal self which the Bible speaks of as "soul" or "spirit." The Scripture presents man as an integrated whole of body, soul, and spirit, not as three isolated components.

Soul emphasizes the distinctiveness of a person's conscious selfhood, his awareness of who he is. It encompasses the entire human being in all his physical life, as in his need for food and clothing. The soul also indicates the feelings, wishes, and the will of humans.

Spirit can be used to speak of both God and man. Spirit focuses on man's derivation from God and thus his utter dependence. Spirit is related to a wide variety of human functions including thinking, understanding, emotions, attitudes, and intentions. The spirit is connected with sorrow, anguish, anger, fear, and joy. In the realm of the spirit God's Holy Spirit grants new life to man and indwells the believer, communicating truth and producing His own character in human life (Gal. 5:22-23).

Body. The embodiment of the soul in human flesh is important to God's design and purpose. Through the body we experience the world, enjoy and control things around us, and relate to other people. The body is our instrument for serving God on earth. In its original design the body was neither evil nor corruptible. Only the introduction of sin caused the physical ailing and aging that ultimately leads to death (Gen. 2:17; 3:19, 22). Sin impacts humans in their entire being, both psychologically and physiologically. Thus man struggles with disordered desires as well as mental and physical issues. At death the soul will leave the present body behind, but Scripture teaches the redemption of the body. While we know that the future body will have some continuity with the present body, we do not know the exact nature of our glorified body (1 Cor. 15:35-49).

MAN IN GOD'S IMAGE

God's image is equally shared by man and woman. The complementary nature of the two genders is designed to lead to enriching cooperation in managing and replenishing the earth (Gen. 2:18-23).

The complementary roles of man and woman in God's image are not simply fulfilled in marriage and procreation but in the wider activities of service to God.

While the Genesis narrative doesn't fully explain what it means for man to be created in God's image, the context gives us sufficient evidence to make reasonable conclusions. We are relational, rational, and responsible. Persons are designed to live in dynamic relationship with each other. God declares, "It is not good for man to be alone" (Gen. 2:18). We demand and desire the fellowship of others like ourselves. Thus the union of one man and one woman is the absolute standard (2:24).

But our greatest relational need is to live in intimacy with our Creator. In the innocence of the garden, the man and woman experienced immediate communion with God (Gen. 3:8). Man cannot live fully without God because we were created by Him and for Him.

Man is *rational*. Simply stated, we have been created with the ability to understand and respond to God as He reveals Himself to us. The garden was designed to foster the full development of man's spiritual, physical, and aesthetic appetites. For the spiritual dimension man was given a word which contained both permission and restriction. He could eat of every tree but one: the tree of the knowledge of good and evil (2:16-17). This command was for man alone because he alone was created with the capacity to hear and respond to God.

Man is also *responsible*. God's first words to the man and woman were words of blessing followed by the assignment to fill the earth and subdue it. Man is God's steward and thus becomes accountable for managing the Creator's resources according to His purpose and standards. Man's freedom does not negate his responsibility toward the one who created him in His own image; rather, it provides the vehicle for man to express his devotion, gratitude, and service to his Maker.

GOD'S PRIESTLY REPRESENTATIVES

As His stewards over all other created things, we are God's representatives on planet earth. After the exodus from Egyptian bondage, Israel stood before God to receive their commission: "You shall be to Me a kingdom of priests and a holy nation" (Exod. 19:6). In the New Testament, Paul speaks of redeemed man as an ambassador for Christ (2 Cor. 5:20). Man's purpose is to advance God's kingdom by His power for His glory to the ends of the earth.

FOR MEMORY AND MEDITATION

"God created man in His own image, in the image of God He created him; male and female He created them" (Gen. 1:27).

i BELIEVE

IN THE FALL OF MAN

The fall refers to the first sin of Adam and Eve, which resulted in judgment upon both nature and mankind. The New Testament writers agree that humans and nature groan from the impact of sin, longing for redemption (Rom. 8:19-23). When Paul compares Adam with Christ, he argues that sin and death gained entrance into the world through Adam, who is pictured as representative of all mankind. All of mankind stands guilty of sin and separated from God because all, like Adam, chose to sin (Rom. 5:12).

ORIGINAL SIN

Man was created male and female in the image of God, placed on earth with both privilege and responsibility. They are to serve as God's stewards over the earth and thus must obey Him (Gen. 1:28). The first humans, Adam and Eve, were given freedom to enjoy the fruit of all the trees in the garden but one: the tree of the knowledge of good and evil (2:16-17). Notice, then, that man is given vocation and freedom as well as prohibition. Vocation and freedom are gifts that imply responsibility, making man accountable. Man is given everything necessary for a complete state of happiness, requiring only that he show fidelity to his Creator and Sustainer.

The tree in the garden stands as a symbol of God's authority, reminding Adam and Eve that their freedom was not absolute but must be exercised within God's guidelines. The issue is this: Will man let God's Word determine what is good or bad, or will he seek to determine this for himself, ignoring what God has said? The prideful rebellion which led the man and woman to partake of the fruit of the tree indicates man's desire to be completely self-legislating. He desires to be like God, possessing absolute independence, accountable to no one, not even God. But such absolute dominion is not the prerogative of man. This kind of autonomy belongs only to God.

The tempter in the story is a serpent who is identified as an instrument of Satan and thus the enemy of the woman's offspring (Gen. 3:14-15). New Testament authors indicate that Satan is the archenemy of man (1 John 3:8, Rev. 12:9). But the presence of the adversary does not negate man's culpability. Man cannot blame his sin on demonic influence. The gift of freedom requires accountability.

It is not insignificant that doubting God's character and His Word is at the heart of man's sin. Adam and Eve questioned whether God had their best interests at heart. This led them to add their own extensions and interpretations to His Word, mentioning to the serpent a prohibition against touching the tree—something God had not said in His instructions to them.

THE RESULTS OF SIN

The results of their sin are immediate and far-reaching. Their sense of shame caused the couple to cover their nakedness and hide themselves from the presence of God (Gen. 3:7-8). Prior to sin they enjoyed an intimate, personal relationship with God, but now shame led to separation from the One who created them and provided for all their needs.

Further, sin impacted the couple's relationship with one another as they began to blame each other for the act of rebellion. The woman's punishment is directly related to her childbearing role which enabled her to fulfill God's command to replenish the earth (Gen. 1:28; 3:16). The man's punishment has an impact upon the earth and its fruitfulness. Now man's toil will be frustrated by thorns and thistles (Gen. 3:17-19).

But I can't leave this story without giving you a glimpse at the hope of redemption. God immediately sought the man and woman who had shamefully hid themselves from His view. He graciously covered their nakedness, even while banning them from the garden. Finally, He promised that the seed of the woman will crush the head of the serpent, a prophecy of Christ's later victory over Satan's arrogant rule.

NEW TESTAMENT APPLICATION

Paul, writing to the Romans, traces the sin problem of all men back to the garden, where our common ancestor Adam chose to sin. Thus, Paul concludes that all mankind is under the power of sin and the reign of death. In Romans 3:9 he states that both Jews and Gentiles are all under sin. Citing the Old Testament, he affirms that "there is none righteous, not even one" (3:10).

Paul states that sin and death entered the world through the sin of Adam and thus are common to all people. Sinfulness now marks everyone from birth; we are born with a nature drawn to sin. Such an assertion does not mean we are guilty simply because we were born into the human race. We are guilty because we choose to sin. "Sin entered into the world, and death through sin, and so death spread to all men, because all sinned" (Rom. 5:12).

Like Adam, all mankind makes decisions concerning what they will do, based on their sense of right and wrong and their own desires. We are free moral agents, but as created beings we are answerable to God for our choices. Tragically, all men have chosen to sin, and thus we stand condemned before a holy God. Yet by His boundless grace and mercy, the tragedy of man's condition has been met with the immensity of God's love.

FOR MEMORY AND MEDITATION
"For the wages of sin is death, but the free gift of God is eternal life in Christ Jesus our Lord" (Rom. 6:23).

i BELIEVE

IN REDEMPTION

Man's rebellion and sin resulted in separation from God, who is holy. This separation can be referred to as "spiritual death." When Adam sinned, he forfeited the intimate communion he had known with God, choosing instead to hide when he heard the sound of God walking in the garden (Gen. 3:8). But the next verse indicates that God called out to man. God is all-knowing and certainly did not require information concerning Adam's location. God was initiating the redemptive process to bridge the chasm Adam's sin had caused.

OLD TESTAMENT

An important Hebrew word used in the discussion of redemption is *kipper,* meaning "cover." It is the word from which "Kippur" is derived in the Jewish observance of "Yom Kippur." The Day of Atonement was the most sacred of all the holy days in the life of Israel. The high priest entered the inner sanctuary of the temple to make sacrifices for the sins of the entire nation (Lev. 16:16-28). The ritual included offering one goat as a sin offering while another was offered alive as a scapegoat.

The primary act of redemption in the Old Testament was the deliverance of Israel from slavery in Egypt. God declares: "I will deliver you from their bondage. I will also redeem you with an outstretched arm" (Exod. 6:6). The death angel passed over the households of the Israelites marked by the blood of the unblemished sacrificial lamb. God delivered His people from slavery, taking them safely through the Red Sea.

Redemption is the act of buying back that which formerly belonged to the purchaser. The people of Israel belonged to God by creation, but by delivering them from Egyptian bondage, they became His by virtue of redemption. One of the most moving pictures of redemption in the Old Testament is found in the story of the prophet Hosea, who "buys back" his unfaithful wife, Gomer.

NEW TESTAMENT

New Testament authors employed images from the Old Testament in presenting redemption through Jesus Christ. Upon seeing the Messiah, John the Baptist, declared, "Behold, the Lamb of God who takes away the sin of the world!" (John 1:29). When Jesus celebrated the Passover with His disciples, He talked openly about His impending death (John 13). His death would enable Him to prepare a place for His disciples and provide the only point of access to the Father (John 14). His death is the redemption price that atones for the sins of the world and buys back those whom God created.

The apostle Paul exhorts the overseers of the church to guard those in their care since Christ purchased them with His own blood (Acts 20:28). The writer of Hebrews uses many of the images from the Day of Atonement to speak of Christ as the one who offered Himself as the redemption offering. Christ entered through a more perfect tabernacle, offering not the blood of goats and calves, but His own blood (Heb. 9:11-12). Verse 12 states, "He entered the holy place once for all, having obtained eternal redemption."

New Testament writers see the work of Christ as the tool of redemption (Gal. 3:13), the payment of a ransom (Mark 10:45), and the offering of a sacrifice (Eph. 5:2). They allude to sacrifices such as the Passover (1 Cor. 5:7), the sin offering (Rom. 8:3), or the Day of Atonement (Heb. 9). John sees the Lamb praised by a multitude because His blood redeemed people from every tribe and tongue and people and nation (Rev. 5:9-10).

THE SUFFICIENCY OF THE ATONEMENT

The Bible makes clear that the death of Christ was sufficient for all of mankind. He gave His life for the sins of the world (John 6:51), and the Scriptures repeatedly indicate that "whosoever will, may come" (John 3:16; Rev. 22:17). So if God has no "pleasure in the death of the wicked" (Ezek. 18:23) and if His stated desire is that none should perish "but for all to come to repentance" (2 Pet. 3:9), then why are some men "lost" and condemned to hell?

The answer actually lies in passages like John 10 and Ephesians 1. John 10:15 speaks of Christ laying down His life for His own sheep. But note that His sheep are those who know His voice and follow Him (vv. 4-5).

In Ephesians 1, Paul speaks of the blessings found in Christ, which include redemption through His blood, the forgiveness of our sins (v. 7). We must ask, "How does one get in Christ?" Paul tells us, "In Him, you also, after listening to the message of truth, the gospel of your salvation—having also believed, you were sealed in Him with the Holy Spirit of promise" (Eph. 1:13).

The atonement is sufficient for all but is effective only for those who have heard the gospel and have believed. This should give us both urgency and encouragement as we share the gospel with others.

FOR MEDITATION AND MEMORY
"For even the Son of Man did not come to be served, but to serve, and to give His life a ransom for many" (Mark 10:45).

i B E L I E V E

IN GOD'S CALL

We love to receive a call from someone we love. In theological terms a call can be a summons, an invitation, or a commissioning. Our call to redemption implies both ownership and the invitation to kingdom activity.

THE CALL TO REDEMPTION

The first redemptive call was heard by Adam in the garden of Eden. After man sinned and attempted to hide from God's presence, "the Lord God called to the man, and said to him, 'Where are you?'" (Gen. 3:9). An all-knowing God was not seeking information but was initiating the call to redemption.

The call to redemption can be seen in the invitation to the early disciples: "Follow Me" (Mark 1:17). Mark indicates that "immediately He called them" (1:20). The parable of the great banquet in Luke 14:16-24 and the marriage feast in Matthew 22:2-14 illustrate the call to redemption. In both stories the call is issued by the host. When one excuse is piled upon another, the master sends his servant into the highways and along the hedges to compel others to come in so that the house is filled. This illustrates both the intensity of God's call and the necessity of man's response. The parable in Matthew ends with the declaration, "For many are called, but few are chosen" (22:14). "Chosen" is a technical word for the redeemed people of God. Our neat and logical distinctions between a divine call and culpable human rejection of God's offer cannot be imposed on the New Testament. Those who choose not to come are held responsible.

THE CALL TO SERVICE

Redemption indicates a "buying back," and therefore the call to redemption implies ownership. In Isaiah 43:1, God speaks of how He owns His people by creation, then declares, "Do not fear, for I have redeemed you; I have called you by name; you are Mine!" Ownership speaks of a covenant relationship. We are called to salvation, given a name, and made heirs.

Ownership also involves a call to service. We cannot and should not separate the call to redemption and the call to ministry. When God determined to rescue His people, He called Moses to be His chosen instrument though whom He would accomplish His purpose on earth (Exod. 3). Another classic story of calling is seen in the story of Samuel. Hannah dedicates Samuel to the Lord and places him in the care of Eli the priest. Samuel originally mistakes the call of God for the summons of Eli. When Samuel understands that the Lord is calling, he responds appropriately, "Speak, for Your servant is listening" (1 Sam. 3:10). God reveals both His plan and Samuel's role within it. Note that when God determines to accomplish earthly activity, He will issue a call that must be answered by a willing servant.

The call to the original disciples was not only the call to follow Christ; it was also the invitation to become fishers of men. When Christ called persons to follow Him, He indicated that the response demanded that they take up the cross and follow Him (Matt. 10:38). Anyone not willing to do so is not worthy of Christ. The call to redemption and the call to mission cannot be separated. We are saved to serve. We are redeemed to join Him in His redemptive task.

THE CHRISTIAN LIFE IN ITS ENTIRETY IS A CALLING

Paul prays that the believers in Ephesus will have the eyes of their hearts opened so they will know "what is the hope of His calling, what are the riches of the glory of His inheritance in the saints" (Eph. 1:18). We are God's redeemed and called people; thus, we are His inheritance. He has chosen to empower us and work through us. In Ephesians 4:1, Paul challenges his readers to walk worthy of their calling.

The nature of God's calling is described using several different images. It is an upward calling (Phil. 3:14), a heavenly calling (Heb. 3:1), a holy calling (2 Tim. 1:9), one that fills us with hope (Eph. 4:4).

THE BASIS OF THE CALL

The call to redemption and service is grounded in the grace of God. Paul invites Timothy to join him in the work of the gospel with this reminder—that God "has saved us and called us with a holy calling, not according to our works, but according to His own purpose and grace which was granted us in Christ Jesus from all eternity" (2 Tim. 1:9). In Ephesians 2:8-9, Paul declares that man has been saved by grace, not as a result of works, so that no one can boast.

The call to redemption and service demands and deserves man's ultimate response. In 2 Thessalonians 2:13-14, Paul outlines the process of God's choice and calling of man to salvation. How does God call us? And what is required of man? It is through the hearing of the gospel and the response of faith that God's calling becomes effectual in the heart of man.

FOR MEMORY AND MEDITATION
"Oh, the depth of the riches both of the wisdom and knowledge of God! How unsearchable are His judgments and unfathomable His ways!" (Rom. 11:33).

i BELIEVE

IN THE VIRGIN BIRTH

The virgin birth is the belief that Jesus was conceived in the womb of Mary by the miraculous, creative activity of God. Mary became pregnant by the creative power of the Holy Spirit without having sexual relationship.

THE DECLARATION

The word *virgin* is used twice in reference to Mary the mother of Jesus, who was at the time engaged to Joseph. Matthew and Luke provide us with two different but complementary and harmonious witnesses to Jesus' birth by miraculous conception.

Matthew views the account from Joseph's viewpoint. Matthew indicates Mary was betrothed to Joseph and that they had not had sexual relations when Mary "was found to be with child by the Holy Spirit" (1:18). Being a righteous man, Joseph determined to send Mary away in some private fashion so as not to disgrace her. But God intervened, sending an angelic messenger to tell Joseph that the child had been conceived in her by agency of the Holy Spirit and should be named Jesus because He will be the Redeemer. Joseph was to take Mary as his wife, and he kept her as a virgin until she gave birth to Jesus (1:25). It is clear from Mark 6:3 that Mary and Joseph had children after the birth of Jesus. The virgin birth is obviously not about the perpetual virginity of Mary.

The fact that Jesus was conceived by a virgin is the basis for the quotation from Isaiah 7:14, recorded in Matthew 1:23, "'Behold, the virgin shall be with child and shall bear a Son, and they shall call His name Immanuel,' which translated means, 'God with us.'"

Some liberal scholars argue that the Hebrew word *alma* used in Isaiah means "young woman," not "virgin." But *alma* is not used elsewhere in the Old Testament in connection with childbirth. Isaiah could have used the Hebrew word for woman or wife if he was referring to a natural birth. Further, they argue that Isaiah was referring only to a birth during the reign of Ahaz. The immediate historical reference is clear (7:14-17), but the larger context indicates that the prophet's thought is not confined to the current historical situation. The use of "Immanuel" in 8:8, 10, as well as the recurrent theme of a child who will be a deliverer, introduce the Messianic theme that flows throughout Isaiah's prophecy. When the Old Testament was translated from Hebrew to Greek (the Septuagint), the translators used the Greek word for "virgin" in Isaiah 7:14, indicating they understood Isaiah to be referring to more than an ordinary birth.

Luke looks at the virgin birth from Mary's vantage point. The angel Gabriel visits Mary, who is described as "a virgin engaged to a man whose name was Joseph" (1:27). Gabriel tells her she has found favor with God and will conceive a son whom she must name Jesus. He will be great, the Son of the Most High, and will establish a kingdom that will have no end. Mary is perplexed precisely because she is a virgin (v. 34). But Gabriel informs her, "The Holy Spirit will come upon you, and the power of the Most High will overshadow you; and for that reason the holy Child shall be called the Son of God" (v. 35).

THE DOCTRINAL SIGNIFICANCE
The emphasis throughout Scripture is on the miraculous conception of Jesus through Mary without an earthly father. It is clearly a creative act of God accomplished through the agency of the Holy Spirit—a miracle of the same magnitude as the original creation in Genesis 1:1. Any suggestion that this story resembles pagan stories of gods having intercourse with women can easily be dismissed. The tone of the virgin birth is radically different from all such pagan accounts. Further, the patent impossibility of such a concept being accepted in a Jewish context rules against any such suggestion.

The virgin birth of the Son of God squares with the miraculous nature of Jesus' entire ministry. He worked miracles and rose miraculously from the dead. He entered and departed the world by the supernatural activity of God. And while we often use the virgin birth to focus on the divinity of Christ, the early church fathers saw it as a defense of His full humanity. They were facing a Gnostic teaching which said that matter (such as the human body) was inherently sinful.

We cannot assert that the Son of God could not have entered the world through a means other than the virgin birth, but the miraculous birth does indeed point to Jesus' deity. Likewise, we cannot assert that God could not have created sinless humanity apart from virgin birth. Nonetheless, the circumstances of His birth call attention to the miracle involved when Mary, a sinner, gave birth to one who was sinless and did not Himself need a Savior. Jesus is the perfect sacrifice for human sins and thus the savior of Mary (Luke 1:47) and the rest of redeemed humanity with her.[1]

The creative power involved in the birth of Jesus gives us confidence that the same Spirit is at work in our new birth (John 1:13, 3:5-6), causing the equally impossible to occur—a sinful man or woman clothed in the pure righteousness of God.

FOR MEMORY AND MEDITATION

"'Behold the virgin shall be with child and shall bear a Son, and they shall call His name Immanuel,' which translated means, 'God with us'" (Matt. 1:23).

---

1.   For greater detail see J. I. Packer, Concise Theology (Carol Stream, IL: Tyndale, 2001), 112.

i BELIEVE

IN THE INCARNATION

The incarnation speaks of God becoming human—the unity of both divinity and humanity in Jesus of Nazareth. It speaks of one person with two natures—Jesus being both fully divine and yet fully human. The incarnation means that the triune God, without ceasing to be God, revealed Himself to humanity for their redemption by becoming man.

FULLY HUMAN

When we read the Gospels, we see clearly that the writers saw Jesus as fully human. Matthew and Luke provide a detailed genealogy of Jesus as they declare His human descent. He was born through the physical birth process and underwent normal childhood development from infancy to childhood. "The Child continued to grow and become strong, increasing in wisdom; and the grace of God was upon Him" (Luke 2:40 and cf. 2:52). Luke underscores the physical, intellectual, social, and spiritual development of the child, Jesus. As a man He was limited in knowledge and thus needed to learn and develop.

Throughout His earthly ministry, Jesus experienced the same physiological needs as any other man. He experienced fatigue (John 4:6) and thirst (John 19:28). Thus His body required rest (Matt. 8:24), food (Matt.

4:2), and water. He expressed human emotions such as surprise (Matt. 8:10), compassion (Matt. 9:36), love (John 11:5, 35-36), righteous indignation (Mark 3:5), and grief (Matt. 26:37). As a man He was fully dependent on the Father and therefore communicated with Him through prayer.

Jesus called Himself a man and spoke of His physical body and its ultimate dissolution (Matt. 26:26). The events preceding and including His death require that we appreciate the limitations of His full humanity. In the garden He prayed for the physical and emotional strength to face what lay before Him. He prayed with such human intensity that He perspired as one under great strain (Luke 22:43-44). His scourging and death were both real and agonizing (Mark 15:37; John 19:30). When the spear was thrust into His side, blood and water streamed forth. His death was real.

YET WITHOUT SIN

As fully man, Jesus had the capacity to sin, and yet the New Testament writers are in full agreement that He lived without sin. Jesus would ask His detractors, "Which one of you convicts Me of sin?" (John 8:46). No voice is heard! Paul affirms the sinless life of Jesus: "He made Him who knew no sin to be sin on our behalf" (2 Cor. 5:21). The writer of Hebrews elaborates, "For we do not have a high priest who cannot sympathize with our weaknesses, but One who has been tempted in all things as we are, yet without sin" (Heb. 4:15).

FULLY DIVINE

While those who witnessed Jesus' ministry experienced Him as fully human, it became evident to them that He was more than a man. The miracles He performed displayed an authority over creation that only God possessed (Matt. 8:25-27). Perhaps most troubling to skeptics was His claim to forgive sin (Matt. 9:2-8), a prerogative belonging only to God.

Further, it is important to note that Jesus frequently pointed to His equality with God. After the healing of the lame man at Bethesda, Jesus equates His work with that of the Father (John 5:17). The Jews clearly understand the radical impact of Jesus' statement, and thus they begin the quest to put Him to death for such brazen blasphemy (v. 18). In this same context Jesus affirms that like the Father He has the authority to raise the dead and give them life (v. 21). The use of various "I Am" statements found throughout the Gospel of John provides clear indication that Jesus equated Himself with the covenant God who revealed Himself to Moses in the burning bush.

The writers of the New Testament affirm the preexistence of Jesus (John 1:1-2). They accord to Him the honor and worship due only to deity (John 5:23 and Rev. 5:12). He is declared to be the agent of creation, the sustainer of life, the revealer of God, the redeemer and reconciler of man, and the regent of the church (Col. 1:13-23).

Paul, in Philippians 2:5-11, graphically describes the incarnation. He affirms that Jesus existed in the very form of God but voluntarily laid aside the prerogatives of Godhood, taking upon Himself human flesh. His obedience was complete, leading to His death. Yet God highly exalted Him and gave Him the name above every name. Yes, His life, death, resurrection, and ultimate exaltation demonstrate that He is fully God.

THE SIGNIFICANCE

Jesus as the God/Man was qualified to reveal God to humankind. He alone was qualified to represent man to God. The redemption of man from the sin that would prevent him from enjoying a personal relationship with Holy God requires the incarnation. Jesus alone was able to accomplish the mission of salvation because in Him alone was full humanity and full divinity.

FOR MEMORY AND MEDITATION

"And the Word became flesh, and dwelt among us, and we saw His glory, glory as of the only begotten from the Father, full of grace and truth" (John 1:14).

i BELIEVE

IN THE CROSS

The cross is probably the best known of all Christian symbols, though it is often worn as jewelry with little thought concerning its meaning. Crucifixion was the most painful, degrading form of capital punishment in the ancient world. Yet this degrading form of capital punishment became the means for the redemption of mankind and the enduring symbol of self-sacrifice for the Christian disciple.

JESUS SPOKE OF HIS COMING CRUCIFIXION

The crucifixion was neither surprise nor accident. The Gospel writers agree that Jesus foretold His own death. Listen to the calm dignity expressed by Jesus in Matthew 26:2: "You know that after two days the Passover is coming, and the Son of Man is to be handed over for crucifixion."

Jesus declared that His death was a divine necessity. In Mark 8:31, He declared, "The Son of Man must suffer many things . . . and be killed." Notice the use of the word "must." Further, He indicated that He would be delivered by the Jews to the Romans, who would actually be the ones to kill Him (Mark 9:31). In each reference to the crucifixion, Jesus assured the disciples that He would be raised from the dead. "They will mock Him and spit on Him, and scourge Him and kill Him, and three days later He will rise again" (Mark 10:34).

Death by crucifixion might appear to be ignoble, but His would actually entail glory. This theme is particularly captured by John, who continually speaks of Jesus being "lifted up" (3:14; 8:28; 12:32-34). This theme of glory is prominent in Jesus' high priestly prayer recorded in John 17: "Father, the hour has come; glorify Your Son, that the Son may glorify You" (17:1).

THE SIGNIFICANCE OF THE CRUCIFIXION

Each of the Gospel writers adds to our understanding of the crucifixion, looking at it from unique vantage points. Mark portrays the absolute horror of putting the Son of God to death. Yet He saw in the taunts of "save Yourself" a clear messianic prophecy of the resurrected King. "Let this Christ, the King of Israel, now come down from the cross, so that we may see and believe!" (Mark 15:32). In a few days time He would not only come down from the cross, but He would be mightily raised from the dead.

Matthew also underlines the messianic theme, making clear that Jesus was in complete control of all events. Jesus' vindication was seen in the rending of the veil of the temple and the raising of the Old Testament saints (Matt. 27:51-54), which links the cross to the open tomb. This means the last days have now been inaugurated, with the power of death broken and salvation poured out upon man. Luke provides us with a picture of reverence and worship as Jesus prays to the Father from the cross, seeking forgiveness for His persecutors and commending His Spirit into the Father's hands.

John's portrayal is majestic. He underlines God's sovereign control as the cross becomes a throne for the One who has been "lifted up." John indicates that the sign of accusation—"Jesus of Nazareth, the King of the Jews"—was written in Aramaic, Latin, and Greek (John 19:19-20), a universal proclamation of Jesus' messianic identity.

THE THEOLOGICAL MEANING

The theology of the cross was quickly developed by the church. Paul quotes from an early confession in 1 Corinthians 15:3-5: "For I delivered to you as of first importance what I also received, that Christ died for our sins according to the Scriptures" (v. 3). Paul had "received" this truth from others and was now "delivering" it to the Corinthian church. Further, he makes clear that the death, burial, and resurrection were a part of God's sovereign plan "according to the Scriptures."

The early church emphasized three truths concerning the crucifixion: First, Jesus' death on the cross was the fulfillment of Scripture. Second, they understood that Jesus' death was on behalf of man, that He was our substitute. He was "delivered over because of our transgression, and was raised because of our justification" (Rom. 4:25; cf. 1 Pet. 3:18). Third, Jesus' death resulted in His resurrection, vindication, and exaltation by the Father (Rom. 1:4; Phil. 2:5-11).

The cross is more than the basis of one's salvation; it is the central event in history. It is a historical demonstration of God's involvement in and control of human history. Thus the "word of the cross" (1 Cor. 1:18) may sound foolish to man, but it is the heart of the gospel and the focus of the church's mission. It introduces into the Christian vocabulary those words that give our faith its true distinction from all other religions of the world. The cross is our means of "redemption," a word that stresses the "ransom payment" required for the forgiveness of sin (Titus 2:14). "Propitiation" refers to Jesus' death as the satisfaction of God's righteous wrath (Rom. 3:25; Heb. 2:17). "Justification" pictures the results of the cross in terms of legal "acquittal" (Rom. 3:24; Gal. 2:16-21). The cross frees man from his sin—not by the works of our own hands but by the perfect, accomplished work of Christ.

The impact of the cross was such that it forged a new basis of unity between Jew and Gentile, breaking down the barrier between the two (Eph. 2:14-15). It consummated the public defeat of Satan and his demonic hordes (Col. 2:15). Thus it forms the basis for our unity today, yielding the source of our spiritual victory. It is the call to costly discipleship. Jesus repeatedly summoned the disciples to take up the cross and follow Him (Mark 8:34; Matt. 16:24; and Luke 9:23). The symbol of death is our emblem of true life.

FOR MEMORY AND MEDITATION

"For Christ also died for sins once for all, the just for the unjust, so that He might bring us to God, having been put to death in the flesh, but made alive in the Spirit" (1 Pet. 3:18).

i BELIEVE

CHAPTER 17

IN THE BODILY RESURRECTION OF CHRIST

Nothing is more central to Christianity than the bodily resurrection of Jesus. Paul, as spokesman of the early church, was so certain of this historical fact, he declared, "If Christ has not been raised, your faith is worthless; you are still in your sins" (1 Cor. 15:17). This bold declaration is given even more clout when we realize Paul made it while people who were eyewitnesses of Jesus' earthly ministry were still alive. They knew and had seen what had taken place. Jesus' bodily resurrection is not only a declaration of the truthfulness of all His earthly claims; it is also the assurance that man can experience life after death.

NEW TESTAMENT WITNESS

New Testament evidence of the veracity of the resurrection falls into four categories—the empty tomb, the appearances of the resurrected Lord before His ascension, the appearances after His ascension, and the existence and vitality of the early church community.

All four Gospels highlight the centrality of the resurrection by giving evidence of the empty tomb and recording various resurrection appearances. While the accounts differ in certain details, they do not contradict one another. Rather, like four eyewitnesses looking at a scene from different vantage points, their stories corroborate one another (Matt. 28; Mark 16; Luke 24;

and John 20–21). The authenticity of their reporting is further documented by the honest appraisal of the fear and doubt of the early disciples. Not only that, but they admit that the initial testimonies of the women who first discovered Jesus' body missing were greeted with skepticism. Jesus appears twice in the upper room, the second time for the sake of unbelieving Thomas (John 20:26-28). He showed them His hands and His feet and even ate fish with them (Luke 24:43).

During His pre-ascension appearances, Jesus provided many convincing proofs and taught them further about His kingdom (Acts 1:3). After His ascension He appeared to Stephen as this first martyr was being stoned to death by his enemies. He allowed Stephen to see Him standing at the right hand of God (Acts 7:55-56). He later appeared to Saul on the Damascus road, an event that led to his radical conversion (Acts 9:1-6; cf. 1 Cor. 15:8). John described his own post-ascension encounter with the living Lord in Revelation 1. Since the Epistles were written prior to the Gospels, the first recorded account of the resurrection appearances is actually found in 1 Corinthians 15:1-8, where Paul listed the appearances in order.

Taking all of these accounts together, we can list the following facts: 1) The tomb was empty. 2) Jesus appeared to many believing disciples on numerous occasions, teaching the believers about the prophetic and theological significance of His resurrection. 3) Jesus' resurrection was not a resuscitation of a ruined earthly body but rather a transformation, a complete renewing of His original body. This transformation enabled Him to touch and be touched, while at the same time He could appear, vanish, and move unseen from one location to another (Luke 24:31, 36). His was a body of a new kind called into existence by God, one without the constraints of an earthly body. 4) He still lives in and through this body in heaven. It is the prototype of the resurrection body available to all those who trust in Him.

THE SIGNIFICANCE OF THE RESURRECTION

We cannot overstate the significance of the resurrection.

- It establishes Christianity as a religion based in history. The resurrection did not occur merely in the minds of His followers, but in actual time and space.
- It inaugurates the "power" phase of Christ's kingship. He has been granted "all authority," and His dominion extends to all peoples and for all time (Matt. 28:18-20). Paul states the same truth in Romans 1:4, referring to Jesus as the one "who was declared the Son of God with power by the resurrection from the dead."
- It inaugurates a new creation. Jesus died in an age dominated by sin and death, but with the resurrection He entered into a new era where He lives to God (Rom. 6:9-10).
- He now sits enthroned at the right hand of the Father where He makes intercession for believers

(Heb. 1:3-4; 7:25), pouring out blessing on His people (Eph. 1:20-21), enabling His church to complete His kingdom activity.

- The resurrection is the ultimate vindication of the Son by the Father. Although Christ was sinless, He died to sin and has now been raised "according to the Spirit of holiness" (Rom. 1:4). This establishes Jesus as the righteous judge of all men because God has "fixed a day in which He will judge the world in righteousness through a Man whom He has appointed, having furnished proof to all men by raising Him from the dead" (Acts 17:31).
- It assures the resurrection of all persons—some to salvation and others to perdition (1 Cor. 15:12-28).

If you want a highly personal view of what the resurrection means to you, read 1 Corinthians 15. Without it there would be no hope for those who have already died, no forgiveness of sin, no hope in this life or in the one to come. I love the declaration of verse 20: "But now Christ has been raised from the dead, the first fruits of those who are asleep."

How should we respond? That is the focus of our memory verse!

FOR MEMORY AND MEDITATION
"Therefore, my beloved brethren, be steadfast, immovable, always abounding in the work of the Lord, knowing that your toil is not in vain in the Lord" (1 Cor. 15:58).

i Believe

CHAPTER 18

IN THE ASCENSION OF CHRIST

The ascension of Christ refers to His going to heaven in bodily form. The ascension of Jesus marked the culmination of His earthly ministry. It allowed eyewitnesses to see the risen Christ on earth and the victorious eternal Christ returning to heaven to minister at the right hand of the Father, thus giving them confidence to continue in what He had taught them.

Luke provides the eyewitness account: "While He was blessing them, He parted from them and was carried up into heaven. And they, after worshipping Him, returned to Jerusalem with great joy, and were continually in the temple praising God" (Luke 24:51-53). "And after He had said these things, He was lifted up while they were looking on, and a cloud received Him out of their sight" (Acts 1:9). Then two angelic messengers tell them that Jesus, who had been taken into heaven, would return in the same manner.

It is impossible for us to comprehend fully how significant it was that the early disciples were allowed to witness the bodily ascension of Christ. Doubt was replaced with courage; reservation with resolve.

THE SIGNIFICANCE OF THE ASCENSION

The ascension declares that the earthly ministry of Jesus is complete and His atoning work has been presented to the Father (Heb. 4:14-15). This is the moment when the humanity of Jesus is taken up to God and glorified, marking the first fruits of eternal salvation (1 Cor. 15:20). Thus, the ascension assures believers that eternal life is their present and future inheritance. Since the "body of Christ" is no longer visible in time and space, this term can now be used to speak of His people—His church—as well as the elements of the Eucharist (or Lord's Supper), referring to His body in a spiritual sense rather than a literal one.

The ascension is God's act of exalting Jesus to the highest position in the universe. This provides a marked contrast to His voluntary act of humiliation by which He took upon Himself human flesh and became obedient unto death on the cross. "For this reason also, God highly exalted Him, and bestowed on Him the name which is above every name, so that at the name of Jesus every knee will bow, of those who are in heaven and on earth and under the earth, and that every tongue will confess that Jesus Christ is Lord, to the glory of God the Father" (Phil. 2:9-11). The exalted Christ is in charge of all that exists and all that happens. He has defeated the reign of death forever and made eternal life possible. His ascension and coronation issue the call for all to bow before Him in worship.

THE CONTINUING MINISTRY OF THE ASCENDED CHRIST

- The ascension enabled Jesus to prepare a heavenly place for those who follow Him. It assures believers that they will be with Him eternally. "In My Father's house are many dwelling places; if it were not so, I would have told you; for I go and prepare a place for you. If I go and prepare a place for you, I will come again and receive you to Myself, that where I am, there you may be also" (John 14:2-3).

- His permanent priesthood allows Him to make intercession for His followers, thus assuring their eternal salvation. "Therefore He is able also to save forever those who draw near to God through Him, since He always lives to make intercession for them" (Heb. 7:25).

- The ascension allows Jesus to expand His ministry from a geographically limited, earthly dimension to a universal, heavenly one. This mandates that the church respond to the Great Commission by joining the exalted King in the advance of His kingdom to the ends of the earth.

- The ascension allows Him to send the Holy Spirit to become the ever-present Helper of His followers. The Spirit will convict of sin, righteousness, and judgment (John 16:7-11).

- The ascended Christ now pours out blessing upon His people so that the church is equipped to manifest His "fullness" on earth today in the same manner that He did during His earthly ministry (Eph. 1:18-23). Verse 20 speaks of God seating Christ at His right hand in the heavenly places. Verse 21 indicates that He has been exalted above every authority, power, dominion, and name. Christ has been given headship over everything for His church.

- Jesus empowers His church to express His fullness by giving spiritual gifts to men and women, then gifting these individuals to the church. "He who descended is Himself also He who ascended far above all the heavens, so that He might fill all things. And He gave some as apostles, some as prophets, and some as evangelists, and some as pastors and teachers" (Eph. 4:10-11).

- As exalted King, He opens doors of opportunity for those engaged in His mission (2 Cor. 2:12-14) and rescues His servants so that the proclamation of the gospel might be "fully accomplished" (2 Tim. 4:16-18).

- He disciplines and purifies His church so that the church will be effective on earth and reign with Him in heaven (Rev. 3:19-22).

FOR MEMORY AND MEDITATION

"For this reason also, God highly exalted Him, and bestowed on Him the name which is above every name" (Phil. 2:9).

i Believe

IN THE CHURCH

The church is a covenant community of born-again believers, meeting together in fellowship to worship Christ, as well as working together to advance His kingdom to the ends of the earth in preparation for His return.

A CALLED-OUT COMMUNITY

The Greek word for church is *ekklesia*, which means "assembly." In Greek thought it referred to an assembly of citizens in a Greek city. Citizens recognized their privileged status compared with slaves or noncitizens. They assembled to deal democratically with matters of common concern. Early Christians perceived themselves to be citizens of the heavenly kingdom, called out by God for a special purpose. "So then you are no longer strangers and aliens, but you are fellow citizens with the saints, and are of God's household" (Eph. 2:19).

Ekklesia was used frequently in the Greek translation of the Old Testament for the "congregation" or "called-out" people of God. The use of this term by the early believers, many of whom were Jewish, would have expressed the continuity between the Old and New Testaments. The church came to see itself as the true children of Israel (Rom. 2:28-29). They were people of the New Covenant, as prophesied in the Old Testament (Heb. 8:1-13).

"Church" is used most often in Scripture to refer to a local congregation, such as "the church of God which is at Corinth" (1 Cor. 1:2). However, it can also be used to speak of the entire people of God (Eph. 1:22). Both concepts are true. A person becomes part of the church by virtue of his or her relationship with Christ. The New Testament knows nothing of a believer existing apart from the church. When one identifies with a local church, he or she becomes part of the universal worshipping community, which is permanently gathered in the true sanctuary—the heavenly Jerusalem (Heb. 12:22-24).

IMAGES THAT DESCRIBE THE CHURCH

More than a hundred expressions are used in the New Testament to describe the church, among them the idea of being the Messianic community. Christ's life and miracles on earth proclaimed the presence of the King and the coming of God's kingdom, a kingdom that would be taken from those who reject His Messianic claim and would be given to a new people of God (Matt. 21:43). When Peter confessed Jesus to be Messiah, he was declared to be the apostolic witness upon whom Christ would build His church (Matt. 16:18).

Here's another example: While the church certainly has continuity with the people of God in the Old Testament, it is seen in New Testament thought as a new creation. "Therefore if anyone is in Christ, he is a new creature; the old things passed away; behold, new things have come" (2 Cor. 5:17). Membership in the people of God is no longer a matter of physical birth and is not determined by any social class or category. "For by one Spirit we were all baptized into one body, whether Jews or Greeks, whether slaves or free, and we were all made to drink of one Spirit" (1 Cor. 12:13).

Paul describes the church as the "body" of Christ, speaking of the church's union with the resurrected Lord (Eph. 1:22-23). When Christ died, all those who are "in Christ" died with Him so that they might live in the power of His resurrection (Rom. 6:3-6). Christ's body on the cross is the body in which the church is redeemed and united (Eph. 2:16-18). Paul uses the imagery of the body to explain how Christ gifts and unifies His church, placing each member into the body as He chooses (1 Cor. 12:18).

The church is a "fellowship of the Spirit." The coming of the Holy Spirit at Pentecost fulfills the promise of John 14:18. The Spirit empowers the church for witness and leads it in its mission (Acts 5:32; 13:2). He creates fellowship by enabling believers to produce His fruit in their lives (Gal. 5:22-24). The gifts of the Spirit equip the church to praise God, edify the saints, and witness to the world.

Other images also exist—such as field, building, family, flock, bride, members, the household of God, a chosen race, a royal priesthood, a people for God's own possession—each term illustrating in some particular dimension the majesty and significance of the church. Ministry through the church allows us to live with eternal impact.

THE MINISTRY OF THE CHURCH

The church is marked by worship that demonstrates the lordship of Christ (Heb. 12:28) as well as a commitment to edify believers (Eph. 4:11-16) and to reach the lost. The Great Commission (Matt. 28:19-20) describes the scope and priority of the church's ministry: to disciple the nations through reaching, baptizing, and teaching obedience to all Christ's commands. Since the scope of the task is universal, individual churches must cooperate with other churches to accomplish this task.

Ultimately the church is empowered by the Spirit, who manifests His power by gifting all members for ministry. Through the Spirit's enablement, some church members are uniquely gifted for leadership functions such as preaching, teaching, administration, and the equipping of all members for service. But every believer is given specific, spiritual abilities for joining in the shared ministry of the church. Living, working, and serving as His people on earth is the most significant task anyone can perform. Through His church we find our purpose and participate in His kingdom plan for the ages.

FOR MEMORY AND MEDITATION

"So then you are no longer strangers and aliens, but you are fellow citizens with the saints, and are of God's household" (Eph. 2:19).

i BELIEVE

IN THE SECOND COMING

The Bible teaches that Jesus' return will be visible, physical, personal, and triumphant. It is a royal visit as the triumphant King returns in glory. His return will signal the end of history as we know it, setting in motion radical transformation as He ushers in a new heaven and new earth.

HIS RETURN WAS CLEARLY FORETOLD

Jesus told the disciples that He would return. When Jesus spoke with them concerning His death, He indicated that they should not be troubled by the news. "If I go and prepare a place for you, I will come again and receive you to Myself" (John 14:3). He warned them that they should be prepared for His return (Matt. 24–25).

The two angelic messengers who were present at Jesus' ascension promised that He would return in like manner (Acts 1:11). Paul frequently spoke of Jesus' return, encouraging the recipients of his letters "with regard to the coming of our Lord Jesus Christ and our gathering together to Him" (2 Thess. 2:1). Peter also speaks about Christ's promised coming, warning those who doubt His return. He assures them that the Lord's return is as certain as the Word of God which created the heavens and the earth (2 Pet. 3:3-9).

HIS WILL RETURN BODILY

Some persons have attempted to spiritualize the return of the Lord by suggesting that it has already been accomplished by His resurrection or by the sending of the Holy Spirit. A few think it is simply a reference to our conversion or His promised presence (Matt. 28:20). Such theories and speculations are no surprise. Jesus warned His earthly disciples that there would be misrepresentations of His coming (Matt. 24:4-5, 11, 23-26).

In response to such false claims, Jesus indicated that His coming would be unmistakable. "For just as the lightning comes from the east and flashes even to the west, so will the coming of the Son of Man be" (Matt. 24:27). It will be a clearly visible, glorious, bodily return. "They will see the Son of Man coming on the clouds of the sky with power and great glory" (Matt. 24:30). Note Paul's dramatic description: "For the Lord Himself will descend from heaven with a shout, with the voice of the archangel and with the trumpet of God, and the dead in Christ will rise first" (1 Thess. 4:16).

Speculation about signs and seasons is both unfruitful and distracting. Jesus said, "But of that day and hour no one knows, not even the angels of heaven, nor the Son, but the Father alone" (Matt. 24:36). He indicates that the coming of the Lord will be like the days of Noah, when people were going about the everyday affairs of life, seemingly unaware of the colossal, cataclysmic event that was about to take place.

In other words, Christ's coming will be unexpected. For this reason Jesus tells several parables warning His disciples to serve Him in such a manner that they are prepared for His sudden return at all times (Matt. 24–25).

THE SIGNIFICANCE OF HIS RETURN

When Jesus returns, He will end history, raise the dead, and judge the world. "Do not marvel at this; for an hour is coming, in which all who are in the tombs will hear His voice, and will come forth; those who did the good deeds to a resurrection of life, those who committed the evil deeds to a resurrection of judgment" (John 5:28-29).

Jesus will give His children their final glory. "When Christ, who is our life, is revealed, then you also will be revealed with Him in glory" (Col. 3:4; cf. Rom. 8:17-18). His coming will usher in a new heaven and a new earth. Peter speaks of the heavens passing away with a roar and the earth being destroyed by an "intense heat" (2 Pet. 3:10). But don't despair! For "according to His promise we are looking for new heavens and a new earth, in which righteousness dwells" (2 Pet. 3:13; cf. Rom. 8:19-21).

Those who belong to Christ at His return will see Him and be transformed into His image. "Beloved, now we are children of God, and it has not appeared as yet what we will be. We know that when He appears, we will be like Him, because we will see Him just as He is" (1 John 3:2; cf. Phil. 3:21). The dead in Christ will rise and those still alive will meet the Lord in the air so that we will be with Him always (1 Thess. 4:13-18). We will receive the crown of righteousness (2 Tim. 4:8). We will be joyously reunited with those to whom we have ministered on earth (1 Thess. 2:19).

THE BELIEVER'S RESPONSE

How should we respond to the promise of His return? The Bible teaches that His return should motivate in us a wise, discerning stewardship of all the resources God has given us. Severe condemnation was reserved for the servant who did nothing with his gifts prior to the Lord's return (Matt. 25:14-30). We should live pure and blameless lives (1 John 3:3; 1 Thess. 3:13; Col 3:1-17; 2 Pet. 3:11). We should bear witness of His love and mercy to those who do not yet know Him. The Lord tarries because He desires that all will come to repentance, that none be lost (2 Pet. 3:9).

FOR MEMORY AND MEDITATION

"For the Lord Himself will descend from heaven with a shout, with the voice of the archangel and with the trumpet of God, and the dead in Christ will rise first" (1 Thess. 4:16).

i BELIEVE

IN THE JUDGMENT

At the end of history, God the righteous judge will set all things straight. This necessitates righteous judgment against all sin. When Christ returns, all persons from all times will be raised from the dead and will stand before the judgment seat. Each person will be required to give account of himself or herself to God (Rom. 14:12), who will "render to each person according to his deeds" (Rom. 2:6). Our earthly response to God's revelation of Himself will determine where we will spend eternity.

ALL PERSONS WILL BE JUDGED

Judgment will be universal. All people of all times and places will stand before the righteous judge. "Therefore having overlooked the times of ignorance, God is now declaring to men that all people everywhere should repent, because He has fixed a day in which He will judge the world in righteousness through a Man whom He has appointed, having furnished proof to all men by raising Him from the dead" (Acts 17:30-31). His judgment will extend to both the living and the dead (Acts 10:42), the Christian and the non-Christian (John 5:27-29).

WORKS WILL PROVIDE THE EVIDENCE

God's judgment will be according to our works. "For the Son of Man is going to come in the glory of His Father with His angels, and will then repay every man according to His deeds" (Matt. 16:27). The parable of the sheep and the goats (Matt. 25) indicates that judgment will be based on one's response to those in need. Paul teaches the same truth in Romans 2:6, where he quotes Psalm 62:12, underlining the fairness of God's judgment. The risen Lord declares: "Behold, I am coming quickly, and My reward is with Me, to render to every man according to what he has done" (Rev. 22:12).

But—this is important—none of these passages should be misread to teach salvation by works. Rather they indicate that a person's works (his life) will naturally give evidence to the passion of his heart. Justification may be a free gift of God's grace, but grace received will logically evidence itself in the living of one's life. Notice, for example, the verses that follow Romans 2:6. Those who persevere in doing good deeds are those who seek "glory and honor and immortality" (v. 7). Those who live in selfish ambition and do not obey the truth, choosing instead to "obey unrighteousness," will receive wrath and indignation (v. 8). Fully devoted followers of Christ passionately seek Him and desire the glory of a holy heaven.

In the scene of judgment before the great white throne, men are judged first by whether their names are written in the book of life (Rev. 20:12, 15) and then by the book of works (20:12b, 13). When Jesus declares that the Father has given all judgment to the Son, He specifies: "Truly, truly, I say to you, he who hears My word, and believes Him who sent Me, has eternal life, and does not come into judgment, but has passed out of death into life" (John 5:24). Jesus earlier declared that the Father sent the Son into the world not to judge the world (in terms of condemnation) but to save the world (John 3:17). Judgment will be based on how one responds to the Son. "He who believes in Him is not judged; he who does not believe has been judged already, because he has not believed in the name of the only begotten Son of God" (John 3:18). Those who reject Christ love darkness and manifest evil deeds (v. 19), whereas those who practice truth and come to the Light will manifest deeds wrought by God (v. 21).

JUDGMENT WILL CAUSE A FINAL SEPARATION

The Bible teaches that judgment will be a point of final and irrevocable division between those who belong to Christ and those who do not. At the end of the parable of the sheep and the goats, Jesus declares, "These will go away into eternal punishment, but the righteous into eternal life" (Matt. 25:46). In the parable of the rich man and Lazarus, Jesus reveals that a great chasm has been fixed between heaven and Hades so that no one may cross over (Luke 16:26).

This final separation will reveal the choices made in one's lifetime. When people reject the righteous Son of God sent for their redemption, they bring judgment on themselves (John 3:19-20). This is the essence of Jesus' warning: "Therefore everyone who confesses Me before men, I will also confess him before My Father who is in heaven. But whoever denies Me before men, I will also deny him before My Father who is in heaven" (Matt. 10:32-33).

SALVATION AND CONDEMNATION
Salvation and condemnation are based on one's relationship or nonrelationship to God. The eternal destiny of man is determined by one's failure to worship the God revealed both in creation (Rom. 1:18-20) and in Christ (John 3:36). Thus, a person's eternal destiny is either to enjoy forever God's presence or to be excluded forever from that presence (2 Thess. 1:8-10).

Judgment is sure, serious, just, and inescapable, giving evidence of a righteous God who must ultimately destroy all sin. Righteous God desires that none should perish but all come to repentance (2 Pet. 3:9). The sending of His only begotten Son and the delay of His return are evidence of His longsuffering grace.

FOR MEMORY AND MEDITATION
"It is appointed for men to die once and after this comes judgment" (Heb. 9:27).

i Believe

IN HELL

The Bible holds to a linear view of history, in which an actual beginning in space and time is moving toward a point of culmination. There is coming a final resolution of history when God will banish all evil and establish perfect peace and righteousness. Hell is the final destination of those who reject God's offer of redemption in Christ.

THE TERMS

The three Greek words translated as "hell" in the New Testament are *hades*, *Gehenna*, and *tartaroo*. *Hades* was the name of the underworld as well as the Greek god of the underworld. In the New Testament *Hades* is used to refer to a place of torment as opposed to heaven, the place of Abraham's bosom (Luke 16:23; Acts 2:27). *Gehenna* means "valley of Hinnom." This valley on the south side of Jerusalem was the sight of human sacrifice (2 Kings 23:10) and the worship of pagan deities. At the time of Jesus, it was a garbage dump that burned continually, a place of abomination (Matt. 18:9; Mark 9:43-48). This physical site provided a vivid, though vastly incomplete, picture of the indescribable horrors awaiting those who must endure the actual place of eternal punishment. *Tartaroo* in classical Greek was a dark and doleful subterranean region, the abode of the wicked. It is used only in 2 Peter 2:4: "For if God did not spare angels when they sinned, but cast them into hell and committed them to pits of darkness, reserved for judgment." The thought of hell is vile indeed.

THE REALITY OF HELL

The New Testament teaches that sin has consequences in this life that must be punished after death. Phrases such as "the lake of fire" (Rev. 21:8) and "second death" (Rev. 20:6) are used to portray the horrific fate of those who reject God's offer of redemption. The doctrine of hell requires that we take seriously demonic sinfulness and divine holiness. The Bible teaches:

Hell is unending. "And the devil who deceived them was thrown into the lake of fire and brimstone, where the beast and the false prophet are also; and they will be tormented day and night forever and ever" (Rev. 20:10; cf. Jude 13; Matt. 25:46; Rev. 20:10). Nowhere does the Bible teach a second chance after death or annihilation. The horror of hell is that death itself would be a relief and a release under such torturous circumstances, but it never comes.

Hell is a place of punishment. Numerous images speak of the awful reality of unending punishment. "Fiery hell" indicates the agony of incineration (Matt. 5:22; 13:50; and 18:9), as does the "lake of fire" where those whose names are not found in the book of life will be thrown (Rev. 20:15). Jude 13 describes it as a place of "black darkness," devoid of all stimulation other than pain. The images of "weeping" and "gnashing of teeth" (Matt. 8:12; 13:42, 50) indicate the intensity of the pain. It is a place of destruction (2 Pet. 3:7) and perpetual torment (Luke 16:23; Rev. 20:10). Obviously a person remains fully conscience in hell. In fact, one of the unspeakable agonies of hell will be the awareness that other persons you have influenced in life may be headed for the same destination (Luke 16:27-31), led there by your own example and encouragement.

Hell is the absence of God and all that is holy. "These will pay the penalty of eternal destruction, away from the presence of the Lord and from the glory of His power" (2 Thess. 1:9). We may think we are appalled by the presence and power of evil we see in our present world, but the idea of a place that is wholly, utterly evil and therefore devoid of all that is valuable, pleasant, beautiful, and worthwhile is beyond human comprehension. In truth, human language does not contain sufficient images to convey the absolute horror of hell.

GOD DOES NOT CONDEMN MAN TO HELL

Heaven and hell do not have equal status in the purposes of God. God created man in His own image so that we could enjoy His presence forever. It is not His will that any should perish. "The Lord is not slow about His promise, as some count slowness, but is patient toward you, not wishing for any to perish but for all to come to repentance" (2 Pet. 3:9). Hell is a destiny that involves the free will of man. J.I. Packer writes: "All receive what they actually choose, either to be with God forever, worshipping him, or without God forever, worshipping themselves."[1] People go to hell because they reject their true destiny.

Hell was prepared for the devil and his angels (Matt. 25:41; Rev. 20:10), but it will also be the final destination of those who love darkness rather than light, those who ultimately reject the righteous Son of God who came for the redemption of all who would receive Him (John 3:18-21; Rev. 1:18). May the images of hell be sufficiently frightening to cause the vilest sinner to flee to the grace of God and dwell with Him eternally.

FOR MEMORY AND MEDITATION
"And if anyone's name was not found written in the book of life, he was thrown into the lake of fire" (Rev. 20:15).

---

1.   J. I. Packer, *Concise Theology* (Carol Stream, IL: Tyndale House, 2001), 263.

i BELIEVE

IN HEAVEN

Heaven is the present abode of God and the ultimate destination of those who by virtue of their spiritual rebirth are Christ's people.

HEAVEN DURING EARTHLY HISTORY

God created the heavens as well as the earth (Acts 4:24), and therefore they are both under His lordship (Matt. 11:25). Until the return of Christ and the establishment of the new heaven and new earth, heaven is the dwelling place of God and His angels (Matt. 6:9). It is the location of His throne (Ps. 2:4) and the seat of His presence. It is the place to which the glorified Christ ascended (Acts 1:11). Since our High Priest understands our weaknesses and has ascended into the heavens, we can draw near with confidence, finding grace in our time of need (Heb. 4:14-16).

Paul pictures the exalted Christ seated at the right hand of the Father, pouring out blessing upon His church. "Blessed be the God and Father of our Lord Jesus Christ, who has blessed us with every spiritual blessing in the heavenly places in Christ" (Eph. 1:3). When the Father seated Christ at His right hand, "He put all things in subjection under His feet, and gave Him as head over all things to the church" (Eph. 1:22). The heavenly reign of the exalted Christ enables the church to express God's fullness in the world today.

Heaven is where believers go at death to await the final resurrection. Jesus promised His disciples that He would prepare a place for them so they could be with Him forever (John 14:1-3). He taught them to rejoice in this truth: that their names are recorded in heaven (Luke 10:20). Peter speaks of heaven as the place where the believer's inheritance is reserved (1 Pet. 1:4). In Philippians, Paul speaks of death as the departing of earthly life in order to be with Christ (1:23; cf. Luke 23:43).

The most complete discussion of the heavenly existence of believers prior to the resurrection is found in 2 Corinthians 5:1-8. Paul expresses confidence that when our "earthly tent" (our physical body) is torn down, we will have a new "house not made with hands, eternal in the heavens" (v. 1). Yet Paul speaks to the concern of temporarily being "unclothed"—his way of describing the spiritual existence of the believer in heaven prior to the time he receives his resurrected body. Scripture describes things beyond our experience as well as our language. So even though we may not be able to understand it completely, we can say with confidence that at death we pass beyond the limitations of space and time to dwell in the presence of God. This singular truth gave Paul great hope, causing him to be of good courage, preferring at any time to be "absent from the body and to be at home with the Lord" (v. 8).

THE NEW HEAVEN AND THE NEW EARTH

 The ultimate home of the believer is the new heaven and the new earth. This represents the transformation of everything to conform fully to God's perfection. The authors of Scripture were forced to describe heaven with tangible images that man could comprehend. These images speak of eternal and perfect relationship with the triune God, with other Christians, and with the renewed creation in a manner that is completely free of all limitation. Thus there will be the elimination of all deprivations such as hunger, thirst, evil, loss, death, darkness, pain, distress, and conflict (Rev. 7:17; 21:4; 22:3, 5). The unimpeded joy of heaven will come from seeing God Himself in the face of Christ (Rev. 22:4) and enjoying His presence forever.

Believers will enjoy the continued ministry of Christ as the Good Shepherd. He will satisfy our hunger, guide us, and wipe away every tear from our eyes (Rev. 7:17). Believers will continue to serve and worship the King (7:15). This allows for continued growth, learning, and development through all eternity. Our use of God's earthly gifts (time, talents, and treasures) will in some measure determine our level of service and reward in heaven (1 Cor. 3:10-15; Matt. 25). This warns us that any present-day irresponsibility on our part can result in some form of permanent, future loss. It is important to underline that our reward in heaven will be continued service, not merely sitting around on clouds and strumming harps. In everything we do, we will seek to bring glory to the King and to Him alone.

Images such as a banquet (Matt. 8:11) and wedding feast (Rev. 19:9) are used to describe the unending celebration we will enjoy in heaven. Three distinct pictures illustrate the perfection of our heavenly dwelling. It is described first as a "tabernacle" (Rev. 21:1-8). This Old Testament image speaks of the experience of the *perfect presence of God*. Heaven will not contain even the slightest trace of sin or temptation to impede man's fellowship with Holy God. Second, it is described as a "city" (21:9-27; cf. Heb. 12:22-24), yielding an image of *perfect protection*. There will no longer be any need for the gates to be closed. They will remain open for earthly kings to bring the honor and glory of the nations before the only true King (Rev. 21:22-27). The final image is that of a "garden" (Rev. 22:1-5), which indicates the *perfect provision* of heaven.

If you know Christ as Savior in this life, you will experience in heaven the unending joy of rest (Rev. 14:13), service (Rev. 7:15), worship (Rev. 7:9-10; 19:1-5), and fellowship, not only with Christ but with all the redeemed of all time (Rev. 19:6-9).

THE PLAN OF SALVATION

It's as simple as ABC. All you have to do is:

A = Admit you are a sinner. Turn from your sin and turn to God. *"Repent and turn back, that your sins may be wiped out so that seasons of refreshing may come from the presence of the Lord"* (Acts 3:19).

B = Believe that Jesus died for your sins and rose from the dead enabling you to have life. *"I have written these things to you who believe in the name of the Son of God, so that you may know that you have eternal life"* (1 John 5:13).

C = Confess verbally and publicly your belief in Jesus Christ. *"If you confess with your mouth, 'Jesus is Lord,' and believe in your heart that God raised Him from the dead, you will be saved. With the heart one believes, resulting in righteousness, and with the mouth one confesses, resulting in salvation"* (Rom. 10:9–10).

You can invite Jesus Christ to come into your life right now. Pray something like this:

"God, I admit that I am a sinner. I believe that you sent Jesus, who died on the cross and rose from the dead, paying the penalty for my sins. I am asking that you forgive me of my sin, and I receive your gift of eternal life. It is in Jesus' name that I ask for this gift. Amen."

Signed _____

Date _____

If you have a friend or family member who is a Christian, tell them about your decision. Then find a church that teaches the Bible, and let them help you go deeper with Christ.

iBELIEVE SERIES

If you've enjoyed this book in the iBelieve Series, you may want to watch for future books:

CERTIFIED TRUE:
TRUSTING THE BIBLE

EMPOWERED LIVING:
BEING FILLED BY THE HOLY SPIRIT

SECURED FOREVER:
ANTICIPATING LIFE AFTER DEATH

TRANSFORMED LIFE:
EXPERIENCING REDEMPTION

CONNECTED COMMUNITY:
BECOMING FAMILY THROUGH CHURCH

Coming soon to AuxanoPress.com
For other titles by Ken Hemphill,
please visit auxanopress.com/catalog